Norse in the North Atlantic

Norse in the North Atlantic

Ryan Sines

Hamilton Books
Lanham • Boulder • New York • Toronto • London

Published by Hamilton Books
An imprint of The Rowman & Littlefield Publishing Group, Inc.
4501 Forbes Boulevard, Suite 200, Lanham, Maryland 20706
Hamilton Books Acquisitions Department (301) 459-3366

6 Tinworth Street, London SE11 5AL

Copyright © 2020 by The Rowman & Littlefield Publishing Group, Inc.

All rights reserved. No part of this book may be produced in any form or by any electronic means, including information storage and retrieval systems, without written permission from the publisher, except by a reviewer who may quote passages in a review.

British Library Cataloguing in Publication Information Available

Library of Congress Control Number: 2019951660

ISBN 978-0-7618-7172-9 (pbk.)
ISBN 978-0-7618-7173-6 (electronic)

Contents

Preface		vii
Acknowledgments		ix
A Note on Names and Terminology		xi
1	Introduction and Historiography	1
2	Settlement and Society's Beginnings	19
3	Changes in Society and Religion	37
4	Trade and Travel	59
5	Troubled Times and Decline	73
6	Conclusion	91
Bibliography		97
Index		103
About the Author		107

Preface

Vikings. The word often leaves people thinking about attacks on innocent villages, plundering and kidnapping. But the Viking Age was so much more than that. The people who lived in the Viking Age were farmers, merchants, smiths and explorers. They came from Scandinavia but spread throughout most of the Western World. They discovered new lands throughout the North Atlantic, including Iceland and Greenland.

The settlers in Iceland and Greenland attempted to create an idealized version of society, much of which was based on their experiences in Norway. Both countries faced different challenges as they developed, and ultimately Iceland survived while Greenland failed sometime in the fifteenth century. Each country, though unique, developed along the same pattern and had many similar characteristics. Iceland and Greenland both dealt with the introduction of Christianity, an overbearing Norwegian king who succeeded in the thirteenth century of annexing both countries, and the effects of environmental and climactic changes in the fourteenth and fifteenth centuries. Society also flourished in the North Atlantic as did travel and trade, with Icelanders and Greenlanders reaching as far as the Byzantine Empire. The Greenlanders continued to travel west, reaching the shores of North America around the year 1000, the effects of which are still trying to be understood. The settlement of Iceland and Greenland offers an analysis of two countries that shared much in common, but only one survived.

Acknowledgments

None of this would have been possible without my wonderful wife, Pam. Your love, support, and encouragement are impossible to measure and equally impossible to live without. And to my two wonderful children who have grown so much faster than this book, Zachary and Madelyn, never stop learning. Someday when you are much older, you will discover how much joy the world offers when you learn more about it.

I would like to thank the history giants whose shadows I get to enjoy, including the many great scholars referenced in this book. Dr. Susan Mobley was instrumental in helping me find the fun in both teaching and learning history, and Dr. Mary Elizabeth Ailes led me into the world of the Viking Age and then let me explore it on my own. Without teachers like you, a passion for learning would become a thing of the past.

Most importantly, thanks to God who makes all things possible. Everything I have and will accomplish is because of His grace and mercy.

A Note on Names and Terminology

In an attempt to make many of the Norse terms and names more readable, many have been anglicized when possible. Some Old Norse terms are used throughout the text because their particular meaning would be too obscured or generalized to convert to English, and this agrees with the form that many of the leading scholars in the field use. For example, a *goði* is best defined as a chieftain who had a network of supporters and voluntary followers, as opposed to a chieftain who owned a large farm and had slaves and freedmen working for him. The term Viking has been reserved mostly for meaning a person who traveled outside of Scandinavia, most notably on pirating or raiding voyages.

I also have tried to be consistent with the particular form of a person's name. Erik the Red, for instance, has been written in a variety of sources by different scholars as Erik, Eirik, and Eric, so even in some quotes I have indicated a change to the form Erik for consistency. Finally, some place names that have well known modern English version have kept the English name when being discussed here, while others that do not have well known English equivalents have been left in their original form. When referencing Greenland, many of the original Norse names are used and not modern Greenland names, and that is due to some uncertainty aligning the Norse places to modern locations. In doing so, it is my hope that this will be more consistent with other scholars and a more readable study, thereby fostering a better discussion on the development of the Icelandic and Greenlandic communities.

ONE
Introduction and Historiography

The Viking Age started in the late eighth century, with a raid on the Lindisfarne monastery in Northumberland in 793 being the first recorded attacks by Vikings in Western Europe.[1] During the Viking Age the Scandinavians spread out in all directions, first raiding and later settling throughout much of Europe and parts of Asia. The expert shipbuilders and sailors of Scandinavia allowed the Vikings to expand their sphere of influence. At the onset of the Viking Age, there were kings and great chieftains throughout Scandinavia, although how much land and influence they had is debatable.

As the Viking Age progressed and chieftains continued to imitate mainland Europe, different leaders began the process of state formation. Denmark was the first Scandinavian country to have a king, with King Godfred being recorded as a threat to Charlemagne around 800. Denmark's first dynasty formed under Gorm the Old and his son, Harald Bluetooth, in the mid-tenth century.[2] Norway's first king to consolidate land and power was Harald Fairhair in the late ninth century. However, after Harald's death his son was unable to maintain power. Unification and Christianization of Norway resumed and continued under Olaf Haraldsson in 1015.[3] The Scandinavian kingdoms not only developed and expanded during the Viking Age, but the Scandinavians also expanded into newly discovered lands.

Two new islands in the North Atlantic were discovered and settled in the middle of the Viking Age. A Norwegian was forced from his homeland and became the first permanent European settler on Iceland, creating a Norse colony that continues to thrive today. Another exiled Norwegian later sailed from Iceland and settled Greenland, attempting to recreate an ideal Norse colony similar to Iceland. However, the Greenland settlement mysteriously failed after five hundred years. The success or failure of Viking Age Iceland and Greenland is directly linked to the settlers' ability to adapt to changes in culture, trade, agriculture, and even religion. Greenland's Norse settlements were disastrous because they were modeled after Iceland's thriving settlement, but failed to adjust to constant economic and cultural changes.

There are a surprising number of similarities between the two colonies, offering fertile grounds for research and comparison. The experiments in civilization in Iceland and Greenland present a variety of scholars—including historians, archaeologists, ecologists, and anthropologists—with raw data on how humans interact in new environments, how Europeans dealt with frontier societies and new lands, and why civilizations fail or succeed. Both islands were virtually uninhabited when the Norwegians first arrived and settled, allowing the settlers to focus on their farms and survival rather than manage conflicts with outside groups. Despite having rare insight into the settlement and development of these countries from their respective beginnings, little has been done to compare them. This study compares the Norse settlements of Greenland and Iceland during the Middle Ages in order to identify key factors in the settlements' successes and failures.

Those key factors are best understood by comparing different aspects of Greenland and Iceland side by side. Chapter 2 details the settlement, push and pull factors for the immigrants, and agricultural lifestyles of both islands' early settlers. The consolidation of power and the attempted unification of Norway under King Harald Fairhair forced many people to leave their homes and livelihoods for the newly discovered Iceland. The power struggles continued in Iceland, forcing some to leave for the even more recently discovered Greenland. Chapter 3 focuses on how society was structured and how it changed throughout the Commonwealth period, but also includes a description of the chieftaincy system, which was the basis for power and honor. Feuding was an important aspect of life in this system and lead to the consolidation of power into the hands of only a few Icelanders. Major power shifts started occurring when Iceland and Greenland converted to Christianity, which is also described in Chapter Three.

The next two chapters shift the focus from mostly domestic issues within the settlers' control to issues outside their control, mainly international communication and a changing environment. Chapter 4 discusses the vital importance of contact, communication and trade with other European countries as well as areas in North America—nearly five centuries before Columbus sailed across the Atlantic. Iceland and Greenland depended on outside trade for many basic goods needed for maintaining their lifestyles, and both suffered as trade frequency declined. Chapter 5 analyzes different theories regarding the collapse of the Greenland colony and determines the most likely causes for Greenland's failure, and it also analyzes how Iceland survived. Theories on Greenland's fate range from climate change to war and invasion, although some will be shown to have much more convincing evidence than others. Chapter 6 offers final comparisons and conclusions based on evidence described and discussed throughout the previous chapters. This structure offers the best analysis of the data and information and also helps identify the key factors that led to Iceland's survival and Norse Greenland's extinction.

The most readily available sources for studying the development of Iceland and Greenland during the Middle Ages are the Medieval Icelandic sagas. These sagas are also extremely controversial and have a rather unique history all their own. The sagas can be divided into three categories: historical narratives, the family sagas, and the Sturlunga sagas. The historical narratives are the *Landnámabók* (The Book of Settlements) and *Íslendingabók* (The Book of the Icelanders), as well as a set of Icelandic laws known as *Grágás*.[4] The family sagas contain more than thirty major sagas and cover the tenth and eleventh centuries.[5] The Sturlunga sagas deal with the years 1120 to the end of the Commonwealth about 1264.[6]

Outside of Iceland, the family and Sturlunga sagas were mostly ignored as historical sources into the middle of the twentieth century, with only the historical narratives being acceptable sources. In Norlund's 1936 *Viking Settlers in Greenland*,[7] he makes scant use of anything saga related. In chapter 4 he hesitantly references travel to Vinland and suggests it is along the Canadian coastline, but that is followed with the statement "we cannot attach much practical importance to the discovery of the North American coastal regions."[8] Beyond that very few references are made to the sagas, especially the Greenland and Vinland sagas, until the identification of L'Anse aux Meadows site in 1960 by Helge and Anne Steine Ingstad.[9] Having used the sagas as a guide, the archaeological evidence then supported the sagas as containing some amount of truth. Historians of Iceland and Greenland became much more willing to cite sagas as sources. Finn Gad, first publishing his monumental *History of Greenland*[10] in 1967, uses sagas as primary sources much more frequently than previous historians. By 2000, Gisli Sigurðsson writes that the sagas "are the major source of information about Scandinavian history in the Middle Ages."[11]

As the sagas became more popular outside purely literary circles and entered primary source discussions among historians, their validity was soon questioned. Jon Viðar Sigurðsson describes three groups of historians and their interpretations of the sagas. Although his description originally applied to the first three decades of the twentieth century, the arguments are mostly the same today and the labels therefore still apply. The first group, the free-prose theorists, "maintain that the Sagas of Icelanders were preserved unchanged in oral tradition, with only minor changes from the time of the events they describe in the tenth and early eleventh centuries until they came to be written down in the thirteenth."[12] In other words, this category of historian believes the sagas are an accurate portrayal of Iceland's Saga Age and therefore are reliable historical sources.

Writing around the turn of the twentieth century, Vilhjalmur Stefansson is an excellent example of taking the sagas as mostly true. In his introduction, Stefansson lists the first of his three sources as the Icelandic sagas, and heavily references them throughout his essay.[13] Gwyn Jones is perhaps the best example of recent scholarship employing the free-prose theory. After openly accepting the sagas as sources for *The Norse Atlantic Saga*, he includes translated versions in the second half of the book and further analysis of some major sagas in the appendix.[14]

The book-prose theorists doubt the reliability of the sagas from the Saga Age, particularly because authorship is basically unknown for the sagas. These scholars focus more on who the authors were and less on the time period or events a saga describes. This is mostly because the book-prose theorists argue that the saga authors would mix in contemporary events and their own personal worldview into the story they were telling.[15] This theory does support the sagas as excellent sources for describing the time they were written down, which causes book-prose theorists to do some outstanding—though often fruitless—work on determining who wrote individual sagas or even which scribes copied them. Snorri Sturluson, author of *Egil's Saga*, is the only saga author confidently identified and agreed upon.

Book-prose theorists are particularly concerned about recreating the fourteenth and fifteenth century mindsets in Iceland and Northern Europe, especially regarding the importance of Christianity to the unknown authors or the early scribes who copied them. Alexander Haggerty Krappe is an early example of a book-prose theorist, analyzing sagas in the 1920s. Krappe traced the symbolism of the omniscient weavers that appeared to Daurrud in *Njal's Saga* back to Celtic legends that originated in Ireland, thereby showing the range of cultural diffusion by the time *Njal's Saga* was written down.[16] Orri Vésteinsson fits the mold of the modern book-prose theorists, particularly emphasizing the role of religion. Vésteinsson utilizes a portion of *Ljósvetninga Saga* to show how the role of a priest was often added in to sagas because it better fit the mindset and practices of the saga author or scribe rather than accurately depicting life during the eleventh century.[17]

The third interpretation of saga reliability is the source critic approach, which is similar to the book-prose theorist in the belief that the sagas cannot be used to accurately describe the Saga Age. They recommend only using the historical narratives of *Landnámabók* and *Íslendingabók*, as well as the legal text of *Grágás*.[18] The source critic approach appears to be the least popular of the three interpretations. Henry Ordower is a modern example of the source critic school. He analyzes *Njal's Saga* to demonstrate the fictional aspect of the sagas, but compares the events to the laws recorded in *Grágás* because "the legal system and judicial process form part of the stock material from which the family sagas are constructed."[19]

Because an author can be grouped into one of the three aforementioned categories does not mean they will always accept or reject sagas or other similar Icelandic sources. The *Saga of Olaf Tryggvason* is an example of a surprisingly controversial saga account. On the surface this particular saga should appeal to both the book-prose and free-prose groups of scholars because it is part of *Heimskringla*, whose authorship is generally attributed to Snorri Sturluson. Many of the authors here are accepting of works by Snorri Sturluson because he is one of the only medieval Icelandic authors identified, which also gives historians a better framework for understanding his works. Anders Winroth, who generally fits the free-prose grouping, writes that the saga's author—likely Sturluson—"worked out Olaf's story with great literary skill. For exactly this reason, this version is practically useless for reconstructing Olaf's history."[20]

A completely different approach towards Snorri Sturluson and *Heimskringla* is advanced by Patricia Pires Boulhosa in *Icelanders and the Kings of Norway*.[21] While Winroth accepts the authorship of *Heimskringla* and questions the validity of the text, Boulhosa questions the authorship but accepts that the saga contained real events between rulers and neighbors. Boulhosa writes that "the sagas in *Heimskringla* can provide a wealth of relevant and revealing material for the analysis of the relations between Icelanders and Norwegian kings."[22] Even though there are a number of other interpretations in between Boulhosa and Winroth, it is easy to understand how divisive and debatable the sagas as resources are.

Sagas are not the only primary source material that is the topic of scholarly debate regarding credibility and usage. The Norwegian priest Ivar Bárðarson's account of Greenland[23] c. 1362 also divides scholars on its credibility and therefore its place in historical research. Bárðarson was sent to Greenland in 1341 as a Church official and also managed the Church's lands in Greenland during that time. After his return to Norway, Bárðarson wrote an account of his visit and what he saw, including the abandonment of the Western Settlement. Archaeologist Joel Berglund flatly dismisses Bárðarson's description of the remains of the Western Settlement as an addition by somebody else into Bárðarson's short description. "The section is clearly written by another hand, and it appears to be a later addition . . . without going into a more detailed analysis of the text here, all that can be inferred is that [Bárðarson] travelled to the Western Settlement and that he did not see any of the inhabitants."[24] Thomas McGovern, another noted archaeologist, concludes that Bárðarson's description is quite plausible. "Bárðarson's short account is matched by analysis of excavations carried out between 1976 and 1977."[25]

Regardless of how different scholars interpret sagas and how they present the primary source evidence, an interesting trend emerges. A majority of Scandinavian historians—at least those accessible in English versions—focus predominantly on the social structures of Iceland and Greenland and the development of those societies. Many of the non-Scandinavian historians spend their time analyzing the laws, feuds, transatlantic exploits, and political situations in Norse Iceland and Greenland. The simplest explanation for this general division is the need for Scandinavian historians to explain their own heritage and culture, while cultural outsiders have an easier time explaining migrations, warfare, and politics. Even in *Land Under the Pole Star* Helge Ingstad, famous for his role in discovering the L'Anse aux Meadows site and a leading authority on the Norse explorations in North America, spends the majority of the book describing the people of Greenland and how they likely behaved and interacted.[26]

Since the saga evidence can be controversial, historians of the North Atlantic need to rely heavily on a range of disciplines and a variety of experts. Archaeology appears the most helpful in trying to piece together the settlement puzzles, especially as archaeology can help defend or refute information in different sagas. Thomas McGovern is a leading contributor to North Atlantic archaeology and works to share recent research and scholarship on Norse societies through his North Atlantic Biocultural Organisation.[27] Much of McGovern's early work regarding Greenland focused on climate change as the major reason for the collapse of the colony, which is still a prevailing view among many researchers. Lately McGovern's work is shifting into a more interdisciplinary approach, including climate change as one of several contributing factors to the collapse. In a 2007 article, McGovern writes with Dugmore and Keller that "unfavorable economic changes and falling population might actually have been the key factors in increasing the settlements' vulnerability to extinction,"[28] although climate change was still a driving factor.

A recent trend in the North Atlantic and Norse archaeology fields has been the publication of archaeologists' essays in book form. Two of the best compilations of essays came in conjunction with the millennial anniversary of contact between the Norse and the native tribes along the North American coast around 1000 A.D. Fitzhugh and Ward edited a massive text to accompany the Smithsonian's exhibit by the same name, *Vikings: The North Atlantic Saga*.[29] Thirty-one essays, mostly from archaeologists, combine with approximately 250 photographs and drawings to tell the story of Viking Age settlements and explorations. The sheer size of the book can be daunting, but a clear organization and a lot of images are beneficial to the target audience of the general public, not necessarily historians and other researchers.

James Barrett edited *Contact, Continuity, and Collapse: The Norse Colonization of the North Atlantic*, another excellent archaeological introduction into the Norse sites. Barrett's collection of nine essays and approximately fifty images and illustrations is intended less for the general public than researchers. In his introduction, Barrett's hope is "that this book will be read as an archaeological contribution to an interdisciplinary debate."[30] These archaeological collections help condense and organize a lot of the information that is scattered throughout various journals and articles.

Annette Kolodny, though neither historian nor archaeologist by training, does a masterful job of comparing the Icelandic sagas on Vinland with Native American stories of early contacts with Europeans. She goes well beyond her Ph.D. in early American literature to interview tribal leaders and analyze different pieces of historical evidence in order to establish the sagas as the first written accounts of life in North America. In a thoroughly engaging read, *In Search of First Contact* argues for wider recognition of Norse discoverers of the Americas and, more importantly, that the contact between Norse and Natives created a lasting connection between continents and was also a precursor to the exploitation of Native Americans.[31]

James Robert Enterline represents another non-traditional field adding to the historical conversation regarding early European contacts with North America. Enterline is a mathematician and computer scientist, but also researches cartography extensively. In a way, *Erikson, Eskimos and Columbus*[32] is a follow-up to his 1972 book *Viking America*.[33] *Erikson, Eskimos and Columbus* offers detailed analysis of a variety of maps in the Middle Ages, many supposedly depicting aspects of North America. Enterline demonstrates that knowledge of North America entered mainland Europe and even Asia. His idea becomes extreme when he writes "divulgence-hiding paradigms can explain *every* instance of apparently fantastical, otherwise unexplained shapes in the Arctic and Far East on maps made after the Thule-Norse encounter."[34] [emphasis in original] It seems nearly impossible to verify all maps made in Europe and Asia over four hundred years as including some shape that was borrowed from Thule tribes. It also implies that the Thule had exact knowledge of the precise shapes which made up North American coasts. Admittedly, this author had problems finding concurrence between the fantastical map shapes and North American geography that Enterline advocates. However, the concept that knowledge of North America spread through Eurasia is plausible.

Despite what medieval cartographers may or may not have borrowed from other continents, Europe continued to expand in the Middle Ages. This expansion in terms of European frontier societies is relatively new and has become increasingly popular since the early 1980s, even though the study of American frontiers became popular after Frederick Jackson Turner's essay a little more than a century ago. In 1988 J.R.S. Phillips published one of the first quality works on medieval European expansion and the resulting relationships with Asia, Africa, and the Americas. Throughout *The Medieval Expansion of Europe* Phillips creates a strong foundation for historians to build on.[35] Because Phillips presents almost a survey format of Europe's expansion, many topics are covered briefly and therefore seem incomplete—or at least setting the stage for further developments.

An interesting contrast appears between Phillips and Enterline. Enterline tries demonstrating those connections between Europe and North America through maps, while Phillips states several times that "there is no evidence that the existence of Vinland was ever widely known outside Scandinavia and its Atlantic outposts in Iceland and Greenland, and the knowledge consequently had little or no influence on the new phase of Atlantic exploration which began during the fifteenth century."[36] Enterline also defends the Yale Vinland map by attempting to discredit each claim of forgery. The Yale Vinland map was discovered in the 1950s, and purportedly claims to be an early fifteenth century map showing the Canadian coastline. Supporters of the map, like Enterline, claim it was at the Council of Basel in the 1430s, while opponents claim it a forgery because evidence of twentieth century materials appears in ink tests done on the map.[37] Enterline writes that he "will proceed to take the map seriously, even while acknowledging that authenticity is still not (and probably could never be) absolutely proven."[38] Phillips lumps the Yale Vinland map in with other fictional stories that purport to show widespread European knowledge of the Norse colonies. He summarizes that point by writing "when stories such as these and the forged Vinland Map are eliminated, it is clear that there was little or no knowledge in late medieval Europe of the lands which we now know as North America."[39] Phillips attributes this lack of knowledge or understanding of Scandinavia as being connected to the late conversions to Christianity of many kingdoms and countries, which leads him to describe the region as "out of phase with the rest of Europe."[40]

One year after Phillips' *The Medieval Expansion of Europe* was published, Robert Bartlett and Angus MacKay published their European-centered collection *Medieval Frontier Societies*.[41] They included a wide range of frontier societies and different features of frontiers. All of the frontier societies they chose were "characterized by the movement of peoples, contact and often confrontation between two cultures, violence which was sometimes endemic, and the social consequences which flowed from this."[42] Robert Burns, a supporter of Turner's frontier thesis and a contributor to *Medieval Frontier Societies*, notes how difficult the concept of medieval frontiers is and reads like a call for future scholarship. "The significance of hundreds of evolving frontiers in a dozen medieval countries cannot be generally assessed until their individual case-studies have been separately researched and presented."[43] Scholarship has greatly advanced regarding expanding societies and new settlements since the call went out in the 1980s for expanded research on frontier societies worldwide.

A major undertaking in European frontiers is the series *The Expansion of Latin Europe, 1000–1500*, edited by James Muldoon and Felipe Fernández-Armesto. Fourteen volumes are planned, with volume three being specific to the North Atlantic. While admitting that, at least in regards to Europe's economic, political, and social situations, "the Viking advance into the Atlantic had little significance,"[44] Bartlett and MacKay suggest Greenland's settlement pattern is a precursor to many other explorations and failed settlements. Also, Greenland is important to understanding other failing societies because of the various source material, which may not always be present for failed civilizations.

Included in the third volume of *The Expansion of Latin Europe, 1000–1500* is an essay by the archaeologist Christian Keller that demonstrates how little progress regarding the comparisons of medieval kingdoms and countries has really been made since Phillips' *Medieval Expansion of Europe*. Keller briefly compares Iceland and Greenland, but focuses mostly on Greenland as a frontier society.[45] He breaks his essay into a very brief historiography and describes the different approaches to studying Greenland, and then focuses on the settlement pattern and the development of Christianity—belonging to which was considered by many medieval societies an important aspect of being civilized.[46]

Another major topic discussed by a range of historians and an aspect of European frontier societies is the role that Christianity played in both Iceland and Greenland. Anders Winroth describes the conversion of Viking culture as a whole, spending the majority of his book focused on Norway, but also includes a description of Iceland's conversion. Winroth describes the conversion as a politically-driven change based on the giving of gifts as a power-base. Christianity was a type of gift that also solidified connections through baptism and godparents. Using Olaf Haraldsson as one example, Winroth suggests "Olaf's immediate purpose in these baptisms was to reinforce the bond between himself and his followers."[47] Winroth argues that early conversion and a chieftain's goal in spreading Christianity centered around a belief in power over a belief in faith.

Anne-Sofie Graslund looks at the conversion process across Scandinavia and specifically the North Atlantic islands, although her conclusion is far different than Winroth's. Graslund writes "The Viking Age is characterized by overlap of Old Norse religion and Christianity, which was marked by extensive mixing of old and new ideas and people and syncretism or blending of rituals and beliefs. Because the domestic religion was polytheistic, adding Christ as a new god was not a problem."[48] Graslund supports her thesis with evidence of continued pagan practices after the conversion. The Icelanders even had Church approval to continue things such as the killing of female offspring and eating horse meat.[49]

Christian Keller offers a slightly different view of who truly helped convert the Icelanders and Greenlanders. As opposed to the traditional idea that the Roman Catholic Church was responsible for converting and creating churches in these Atlantic islands, Keller suggests the Celtic Catholic Church had greater influence and was more accepted by the farmers of Iceland and Greenland. He concludes "circular churchyards are evidence of a Celtic Christian mission, being a forerunner for, or coterminous with, the mission from the Roman Catholic Church which seems to have favored the rectangular layout."[50] This line of thought has consequences for how the German and Scandinavian bishops interacted and treated the settlements, as will be seen in later chapters.

Orri Vésteinsson focuses solely on the Church in Iceland, although he is less concerned with the Conversion than with the changes implemented by the Church in Iceland's social structure.[51] The change is not immediate nor is it rapid, but the change appears inevitable due to the inherent need for the Church to be organized. Vésteinsson establishes that "it took a long time for the Nordic church to gain an identity of its own, and that before it did, the Church was simply one aspect of life—an aspect which grew in importance because of its intrinsic need to organize itself and conditions around it."[52] Therefore the Church was responsible, at least in part, for changing society and who had power in Medieval Iceland. This change due to the Church, Vésteinsson argues, is a key reason Iceland ended up submitting to Norway in the thirteenth century.

Sharing part of the concepts of both Winroth and Vésteinsson is the theory developed by Jon Viðar Sigurðsson. While he agrees that Christianity's organization helped create a social structure similar to a mainland European kingdom, and that it worked from the top down, his focus is instead on the power that social structure gave to chieftains after the conversion and the growth of the Church. "The relationship between secular and spiritual power did not change significantly with the introduction of Christianity. One might say there was a Christian-cult basis instead of a heathen-cult one."[53] To Sigurðsson, the chieftain was the guardian of religion both before and after the conversion, which equated to power and prestige if done right.

Jesse Byock also spends time discussing the role of the Church in Icelandic society, most of which dealing with the cultural impact the Church had, although he recognizes the Church as a source of power for chieftains as well. Byock describes the rise to power of some chieftains as a result of their opposition to the Church, until the tithe law came into effect and gave church-owners another source of income through which they could reinforce their status.[54] The cultural influences were mostly educational, although Byock does not connect these changes to the need for submission to Norway.

It should be noted that nearly all the conversation regarding conversion and the Church in the North Atlantic islands focuses on Iceland, rarely including Greenland in much detail. Most historians dealing with Christianity in Greenland focus less on the growth or impact of the

Introduction and Historiography

Church but instead use Christianity to illustrate the poor connections between Greenland and the European continent. This is undoubtedly due to the lack of source material from Greenland and the wealth of misinformed information from continental sources. Poul Norlund focuses most of his description of Greenland's Christianity on the formation of physical church structures. While some believe the Church in Iceland changed the power structure and aided in Iceland's decline, Norlund finds the Church a contributing factor for making the Greenland community last so long. "The Church, the ecclesiastical organization, became one of the bonds which most firmly united those remote settlements with Europe and so with the whole of the civilized world; without those ties they could not have preserved their vitality so long."[55]

Norlund is not only one of the first to study the role of the Church in Greenland, he is also one of the earliest to study and write about Medieval Greenland. He was one of the first modern archaeologists to work in Greenland, excavating around Herjolfsnes between 1921 and 1932.[56] Understandably, his work is very level-headed and fact based, an expert archaeological view with a tendency towards the role nature played in settling and surviving Greenland. While a book-prose theorist and not heavily reliant on sagas, Norlund's thorough survey of Norse Greenland remarkably identifies the likely sites of the Norse-related places along the Canadian coast a quarter of a century before any tangible evidence was found by the Ingstads at L'Anse aux Meadows.[57]

Helge Ingstad is also an archaeologist but with a strong belief in the sagas, as seen in *Land Under the Pole Star*.[58] Ingstad—though wordy—describes an enchanting scene of Greenland in the Viking Age, even while he explains the journey he and his wife take through Greenland. A leisure reader certainly enjoys *Land Under the Pole Star* for the breathtaking descriptions Ingstad offers, but there is still a lot of wide-ranging and valuable information found amongst the stories. The passion carried by the words of Ingstad likely derive from his exploration of the country and a love for knowledge, but he also makes the settlers seem nearly infallible if not for the fact their settlements declined until they were wiped out one way or another. Ingstad's work is still very wide ranging and he is most certainly an expert in the Viking voyages and settlements of the North Atlantic.

One of the things that makes Finn Gad's work on Greenland stand out is that he actually lived there, which provides extra and unique insights. Another stand out feature is the sheer size of Gad's project. His goal in the *History of Greenland* is to "follow a description of economic, social and cultural development in Greenland."[59] The majority of the first volume deals with Inuit and other tribes until the reappearance of Europeans, although he does include a chapter on Norse settlement and two on the decline of the Norse civilization in Greenland. His theories and conclusions, similar to Norlund and Ingstad, are based on the emerging archaeological work in Greenland, which recently has taken some momentous leaps forward.

Today a plethora of scholars and archaeologists are working in various sites throughout Greenland, including Keller, McGovern, and Berglund. Berglund is most famous for the "Farm Beneath the Sand" site found in 1990, which will be discussed in depth later.[60] He has also continued to offer convincing evidence and support for a theory of decline based on the failure of the Norse settlers to adapt to changing conditions—whether climatic or agricultural. Therefore, the blame is mostly on the settlers, especially since other groups, like the Inuit, did survive those changes.[61] Keller and McGovern mostly focused on climate change as the main cause for Norse decline in Greenland.[62] That view is beginning to change in recent publications. While climate change is still an extremely important variable, it is no longer necessarily the only variable that changed in Greenland. Fluctuating trade patterns and economic changes are now being considered as other vital changes that led to the Greenlanders' decline and extinction.[63]

Niels Lynnerup offers a different explanation for what happened to the Norse Greenlanders. Lynnerup creates a unique vantage point on the topic because he writes from a forensic scientist's and anthropologist's point of view. While his analysis of skeletal remains in church graves is extraordinarily in depth and precise, his conclusion deserves particular mention. The Greenlanders, in Lynnerup's studied opinion, "gave up some land and fjords that had become less and less profitable for their way of life and moved back to more auspicious shores where new opportunities had arisen."[64] The last written account of Greenland—focused on a wedding in 1408—mentions the young couple moved to Iceland, which agrees with Lynnerup's assertions.

Compared to Greenland, Iceland is rich in written histories and primary sources—sagas as well as the archaeological record. A large selection of sources and continuing archaeological work allow for a variety of approaches, many of which are mentioned above. That in turn creates a set of leading scholars, including Vésteinsson, Hastrup, Sigurðsson, Byock, Miller, and Boulhosa. Beyond doing excellent work, they are noted here because they all have a range of expertise that allows them to cover a wide range of topics dealing with the Viking Age and the North Atlantic.

Orri Vésteinsson, a professor at the University of Iceland, focuses on the role of the Church in Iceland in *The Christianization of Iceland*,[65] as discussed earlier. He also publishes extensive archaeological-based articles, often times with McGovern, Fridriksson, or Dugmore. Collectively, Vésteinsson focuses on the changes and development in Icelandic society in the Middle Ages. One of his recently published articles, "Expensive Errors or Rational Choices: The Pioneer Fringe in Late Viking Age Iceland,"[66] deals with the societal forces leading to settlement in less-than-ideal places and identifies human factors as causes for settlement patterns instead of environmental forces.

Kirsten Hastrup, a professor and anthropologist in Denmark, also focuses heavily on the role of a changing society in Medieval Iceland and the impact those changes had on the destruction of society. She writes *Culture and History in Medieval Iceland* from the vantage point of a social anthropologist and considers the Icelandic Free State, or Commonwealth period, "a fascinating social 'experiment' created in the wake of Viking expansion, it ended as an experience of conflict and submission."[67] Hastrup works through an extensive amount of social topics—religion, kin groups, social classes, and more—to create one of the most all-encompassing cultural descriptions of Medieval Iceland. In her analysis, the failure of Iceland to maintain order led to the submission to Norway in the thirteenth century.

Norwegian professor and author Jon Viðar Sigurðsson centers much of his work around the political processes in Medieval Scandinavia. In *Chieftains and Power in the Icelandic Commonweatlh*,[68] he follows the development of chieftaincies and how they consolidated control leading up to the 1262/64 treaty with Norway. The chieftain system, he argues, was plagued by "instability throughout the whole of the Commonwealth period."[69] Political developments moved from the establishment of chieftaincies—what Sigurðsson labels as the first phase—towards the establishment of domains—the second phase. The third phase continues with the consolidation of the domains into the hands of a small number of people and ends with submission to Kings Haakon and Magnus.[70]

UCLA professor of history, archaeology, and Old Norse language Jesse Byock tends to show up everywhere in discussions of Iceland and the Viking Age. Similar to Hastrup, Byock covers an assortment of topics ranging from life as a farmer to the role of chieftains, the power of the Church to the legal system, and seemingly everything in between. Byock writes in a narrative style that is in depth yet easy to follow, likely one of the reasons he is a leader in the field. In *Medieval Iceland*, Byock spends much of the time putting forth the concept that a chieftain "did have the opportunity to derive a substantial income from control of a chieftaincy. Because of the manner in which advocacy arrangements dominated the exercise of authority, chieftains were in a uniquely advantageous position to acquire property from bændr."[71] *Viking Age Iceland*, however, covers immigration, politics, trade, the environment, and more in order to increase "our understanding of the social forces and environmental factors which shaped the lives of medieval Icelanders in the period from the tenth to the end of the thirteenth century."[72]

William Ian Miller, a law professor at the University of Michigan, analyzes the social structures and social process as they relate to legal proceedings during the Saga Age. Miller chose Iceland as a study because "Iceland's isolation gives us a society freer from outside impingements than most other European cultures. Its disorders were systemic, not imposed."[73] A leading concept in Miller's *Bloodtaking and Peacemaking* is honor, because "it was by getting even that one established the inviolability of one's honor, that is, by getting even, paradoxically, one person reasserted superiority relative to another."[74] The concept of honor as a driving force in law and retribution appears unique and can easily be oversimplified, but Miller masterfully weaves together legal texts and saga evidence to show how vital one's honor was to the decision making process.

Patricia Pires Boulhosa has a background that makes her uniquely qualified to examine the connection between Icelanders and the Norwegian kings around the time of the submission to Norway. Boulhosa holds degrees in law, history, and Icelandic literature, which she uses to show how the Icelanders negotiated for certain rights and exceptions that were unavailable to other subjects under the Norwegian kings. Boulhosa asserts that those negotiations and even the settlement of Iceland were a result of conflicts with royal power. "The Norwegians who left the country were not seeking to construct a different society in Iceland; they decided to leave their country because they were not allowed to live as their ancestors lived."[75] She also suggests that Icelanders, at least from their own viewpoint, were "the keepers of the ancient Norwegian individual freedom."[76] This is what gave them the power to negotiate their treaty with the king.

Notably absent from this discussion is a focused comparison between Iceland and Greenland during the Middle Ages. With little outside influence, the Scandinavians settled two practically uninhabited islands and attempted to create nearly identical civilizations. Iceland continued to grow and adapt to changes, whereas Greenland struggled to survive until ultimately failing. Greenland was not uninhabitable, even as the climate and environment deteriorated, so the true cause for Greenland's extinction may be more social than environmental. This study will bridge that gap and be a comparison between Iceland and Greenland.

Overall, a lot of the varying interpretations on Medieval Iceland and Greenland deal with what to do with the sagas. The best approaches and most successful arguments use the sagas as mostly true, similar to the free-prose theory, so long as they have other corroborating evidence. This is one of the reasons why the archaeological work that has been done and is still underway is so vital to the growing scholarship on these two Viking Age communities. The facts that are clear lead to differing conclusions—the impact of the Church on the development of society is one example. Each study has strong attributes and adds to a better understanding of Iceland or Greenland, but a conversation comparing the decline of the two Norse settlements will help establish a better understanding of what helps and hurts a society's growth. The discussion that follows will hopefully add to that conversation and foster that understanding.

NOTES

1. Else Roesdahl, *The Vikings* (New York: Penguin Books, 1998), 9–10.
2. Ibid., 73–74.
3. Ibid., 74–75.
4. Jesse L Byock, *Medieval Iceland: Society, Sagas, and Power* (Berkeley: University of California Press, 1988), 15.
5. Jesse L Byock, "Saga Form, Oral Prehistory, and the Icelandic Social Context," *New Literary History* 16, no. 1 (Autumn 1984): 153.
6. Byock, *Medieval Iceland*, 31.
7. Poul Norlund, *Viking Settlers in Greenland and Their Descendants during Five Hundred Years* (New York: Kraus Reprint Co., 1971).
8. Ibid., 89.
9. Government of Canada Parks Canada Agency, "Parks Canada - L'Anse Aux Meadows National Historic Site - History," September 20, 2012, http://www.pc.gc.ca/eng/lhn-nhs/nl/meadows/natcul.aspx.
10. Finn Gad, *History of Greenland: I. Earliest Times to 1700*, trans. Ernst Dupont, First Canadian edition (McGill-Queen's University Press, 1971).
11. Gisli Sigurðsson, "Eddas and Sagas in Medieval Iceland," in *Vikings: The North Atlantic Saga*, ed. William W Fitzhugh and Elizabeth I Ward (Washington, D.C.: Smithsonian Institution Press, in association with the National Museum of Natural History, 2000), 186.
12. Jon Viðar Sigurðsson, *Chieftains and Power in the Icelandic Commonwealth* (Odense: University Press of Southern Denmark, 1999), 20.
13. Vilhjalmur Stefansson, "The Icelandic Colony in Greenland," *American Anthropologist, New Series* 8, no. 2 (June 1906): 262–70.
14. Gwyn Jones, *The Norse Atlantic Saga: Being the Norse Voyages of Discovery and Settlement to Iceland, Greenland, and North America*, 2nd edition (New York: Oxford University Press, 1986).
15. Sigurðsson, *Chieftains and Power in the Icelandic Commonwealth*, 20.
16. Alexander Haggerty Krappe, "The Valkyrie Episode in the Njals Saga," *Modern Language Notes* 43, no. 7 (November 1928): 473.
17. Orri Vésteinsson, *The Christianization of Iceland: Priests, Power, and Social Change 1000-1300* (Oxford: Oxford University Press, 2000), 30.
18. Sigurðsson, *Chieftains and Power in the Icelandic Commonwealth*, 20.
19. Henry Ordower, "Exploring the Literary Function of Law and Litigation in 'Njal's Saga,'" *Cardozo Studies in Law and Literature* 3, no. 1 (April 1991): 41, doi:10.2307/743501.
20. Anders Winroth, *Conversion of Scandinavia: Vikings, Merchants, and Missionaries in the Remaking of Northern Europe* (New Haven, CT: Yale University Press, 2014), 124.
21. Patricia Pires Boulhosa, *Icelanders and the Kings of Norway: Mediaeval Sagas and Legal Texts* (Leiden: Brill Academic Pub, 2005).
22. Ibid., 32.
23. Ivar Bárðarson, "A Fourteenth-Century Description of Greenland," trans. Derek Mathers, *Saga-Book* 33 (2009): 78–82.
24. Joel Berglund, "The Decline of the Norse Settlements in Greenland," *Arctic Anthropology* 23, no. 1/2 (January 1, 1986): 117.
25. Thomas H. McGovern, "The Demise of Norse Greenland," in *Vikings: The North Atlantic Saga*, ed. William W Fitzhugh and Elizabeth I Ward (Washington, D.C.: Smithsonian Institution Press, in association with the National Museum of Natural History, 2000), 337.

26. Helge Ingstad, *Land Under the Pole Star: A Voyage to the Medieval Norse Settlements of Greenland and the Saga of a People That Vanished*, trans. Naomi Walford (New York: St. Martin's Press, 1966).
27. "NABO: North Atlantic Biocultural Organisation," accessed April 7, 2014, http://www.nabohome.org/.
28. Andrew J. Dugmore, Christian Keller, and Thomas H. McGovern, "Norse Greenland Settlement: Reflections on Climate Change, Trade, and the Contrasting Fates of Human Settlements in the North Atlantic Islands," *Arctic Anthropology* 44, no. 1 (January 1, 2007): 29.
29. William W Fitzhugh, Ward, and National Museum of Natural History (U.S.), *Vikings: The North Atlantic Saga* (Washington: Smithsonian Institution Press, in association with the National Museum of Natural History, 2000).
30. James H Barrett, "Introduction," in *Contact, Continuity, and Collapse: The Norse Colonization of the North Atlantic*, ed. James H Barrett (Turnhout, Belgium: Brepols, 2008), 2.
31. Annette Kolodny, *In Search of First Contact: The Vikings of Vinland, the Peoples of the Dawnland, and the Anglo-American Anxiety of Discovery* (Durham, NC: Duke University Press Books, 2012).
32. James Robert Enterline, *Erikson, Eskimos, and Columbus: Medieval European Knowledge of America* (Baltimore: Johns Hopkins University Press, 2004).
33. James Robert Enterline, *Viking America: The Norse Crossings & Their Legacy* (Garden City, NY: J. R. Enterline, 1972).
34. Enterline, *Erikson, Eskimos, and Columbus*, 73–74.
35. J. R. S. Phillips, *The Medieval Expansion of Europe* (New York: Oxford University Press, 1988).
36. Ibid., 164.
37. Jessica Gorman, "Questions of Origin," *Science News* 162, no. 7 (August 17, 2002): 109, doi:10.2307/4013794.
38. Enterline, *Erikson, Eskimos, and Columbus*, 63.
39. Phillips, *The Medieval Expansion of Europe*, 182.
40. Ibid.
41. Robert Bartlett and Angus MacKay, *Medieval Frontier Societies*, Reprint (New York: Oxford University Press, 2011).
42. Ibid, vii.
43. Robert I. Burns, "The Significance of the Frontier in the Middle Ages," in *Medieval Frontier Societies*, ed. Robert Bartlett and Angus MacKay, Reprint (New York: Oxford University Press, 2011), 317.
44. James Muldoon, *The North Atlantic Frontier of Medieval Europe: Vikings and Celts* (Farnham, England: Ashgate, 2009), xvii.
45. Christian Keller, "Vikings in the West Atlantic: A Model of Norse Greenlandic Medieval Society," in *The North Atlantic Frontier of Medieval Europe: Vikings and Celts*, ed. James Muldoon, vol. 3, The Expansion of Latin Europe, 1000-1500 (Surrey, England: Ashgate Publishing Limited, 2009), 25–46.
46. Muldoon, *The North Atlantic Frontier of Medieval Europe*, xvii.
47. Winroth, *Conversion of Scandinavia*, 141.
48. Anne-Sofie Gräslund, "Religion, Art, and Runes," in *Vikings: The North Atlantic Saga*, ed. William W Fitzhugh and Elizabeth I Ward (Washington, D.C.: Smithsonian Institution Press, in association with the National Museum of Natural History, 2000), 61.
49. Ibid., 68–69.
50. Keller, "Vikings in the West Atlantic: A Model of Norse Greenlandic Medieval Society," 37.
51. Vésteinsson, *The Christianization of Iceland*, 1.
52. Ibid., 4.
53. Sigurðsson, *Chieftains and Power in the Icelandic Commonwealth*, 193–194.
54. Byock, *Medieval Iceland*, 148.

55. Norlund, *Viking Settlers in Greenland and Their Descendants during Five Hundred Years*, 30.
56. Ibid., 12.
57. Ibid., 88.
58. Ingstad, *Land Under the Pole Star*.
59. Gad, *History of Greenland*, xiii.
60. Joel Berglund, "The Farm Beneath the Sand," in *Vikings: The North Atlantic Saga*, ed. William W Fitzhugh and Elizabeth I Ward (Washington, D.C.: Smithsonian Institution Press, in association with the National Museum of Natural History, 2000), 295.
61. Berglund, "The Decline of the Norse Settlements in Greenland," 117.
62. McGovern, "The Demise of Norse Greenland," 327.
63. Dugmore, Keller, and McGovern, "Norse Greenland Settlement," 12.
64. Niels Lynnerup, "Life and Death in Norse Greenland," in *Vikings: The North Atlantic Saga*, ed. William W Fitzhugh and Elizabeth I Ward (Washington, D.C.: Smithsonian Institution Press, in association with the National Museum of Natural History, 2000), 294.
65. Vésteinsson, *The Christianization of Iceland*.
66. O. Vésteinsson et al., "Expensive Errors or Rational Choices : The Pioneer Fringe in Late Viking Age Iceland.," *European Journal of Post-Classical Archaeologies* 4 (May 1, 2014): 39–68.
67. Kristen Hastrup, *Culture and History in Medieval Iceland: An Anthropological Analysis of Structure and Change* (Oxford ; New York: Oxford University Press, 1985), 238.
68. Sigurðsson, *Chieftains and Power in the Icelandic Commonwealth*.
69. Ibid., 56.
70. Ibid., 207–208.
71. Byock, *Medieval Iceland*, 222.
72. Jesse L Byock, *Viking Age Iceland* (New York: Penguin Books, 2001), xviii.
73. William Ian Miller, *Bloodtaking and Peacemaking: Feud, Law, and Society in Saga Iceland* (Chicago: University of Chicago Press, 1997), 5.
74. Ibid., 302.
75. Boulhosa, *Icelanders and the Kings of Norway*, 176.
76. Ibid., 193.

TWO

Settlement and Society's Beginnings

The movement of the Norse into the islands of the North Atlantic happened for a number of reasons. Some migrants wanted new land, some needed to explore, and some were forced out by fear of tyranny. Whether they traveled by choice or by force the settlers in Iceland and Greenland attempted to recreate the lifestyle they had wanted in their Scandinavian homelands. The Norse settlers in Iceland and Greenland cared more about creating a permanent settlement rather than creating a base to continue raiding continental Europe and the British Isles—although some settlers did join Viking parties for fortune and fame. Understanding why Iceland and Greenland were settled helps understand how and why they changed from initial settlements of disconnected and independent farms into societies based on laws and structure, as well as understanding why Iceland survived and Greenland failed.

Laying on the edge of the Arctic Circle, Iceland is the result of volcanic activity along the Mid-Atlantic Ridge and contains just under 40,000 square miles of land. However, much of the interior of Iceland is unusable and uninhabited, even today, because of massive inland glaciers. The Vatna Glacier alone covers 2,240 square miles and is nearly 3,000 feet deep. The volcanic origins of Iceland created dried lava flows and layers of basalt underneath much of Iceland's soil and grass. Volcanoes also indicate that the Norse who arrived in Iceland had no real predators to worry about beside the arctic fox, which allowed the settlers' livestock to roam and graze freely. Iceland sits between two currents and two air masses that create climate extremes and unpredictability. The warm Gulf Stream current and warm southern air mass can create optimal farming scenarios, while the East Greenland current and the cold polar air mass bring constant cold to parts of the island.[1] The Viking Age settlers to Iceland also benefited greatly from the Medieval Warm Period, which raised the average temperature one degree Celsius. An increase in the average temperature means a longer growing season and a wider range of crop options than would normally be reasonable.[2] Almost all of the Icelanders' efforts to cope with such a varied climate were recorded in a variety of sources.

The best source available for describing the settlement of Iceland is the written history of Ari Thorgilsson, more commonly known as Ari the Learned, an Icelandic priest writing in the first half of the twelfth century. He is credited with both *Íslendingabók* (*The Book of the Icelanders*) and *Landnámabók* (*The Book of Settlements*). The first is a short account of the settlement of Iceland and names Ingolf as the first permanent settler in Iceland, while the latter is a much more detailed account of the entire *landnám*, or land-taking.[3] While Ari wrote nearly two centuries after the settlement period finished, his work is supported by archaeological evidence and therefore is considered as accurate. Remarkably, despite being a priest and writing after Iceland had officially been Christian for over a century, Ari does not seem to discredit settlers for being pagan and does not write from an overly anti-pagan view.

Ari frames the Scandinavian discovery and settlement of Iceland around the papacies of Adrian II (867–72) and John VIII (872–82) and the reign of Louis the German (843–76). The settlement closes during Gorm the Old's reign in Denmark (died 958).[4] Ari tells the story that the first Europeans to settle Iceland were Irish Christians, which Ari calls *papar*, in the late eighth century and claims that the Scandinavian settlers "found Irish books, bells, croziers and lots of other things."[5] Dicuil, an Irish monk, also describes Christians living in the North Atlantic on the island of Thule—assumed by many scholars today to refer to Iceland. Writing around 825 Dicuil says "it is now thirty years since clerics, who had lived on the island from the first of February to the first of August, told me that not only at the summer solstice, but in the days round about it . . . a man could do whatever he wished as though the sun were there, even remove lice from his shirt."[6] This description fits Iceland, and the time frame— thirty years before Dicuil's writing in 825—places monks on Thule around the end of the eighth century, about a century before the Norwegians settled Iceland.

After Ari references the *papar* he turns the narrative to the Norwegian discovery of Iceland by a Viking called Naddodd, who gave the island the name of Snowland.[7] Gardar Svafarsson then explored the island and found it was "wooded all the way from the mountains right down to the sea."[8] The next Viking to visit the island, Floki Vilgerdarson, gave the land the name Iceland. The story of Floki also creates the first warning of dealing with the North Atlantic environment. "At that time the fjord was teeming with fish, and they got so caught up with fishing they forgot to make hay, so their livestock starved to death the following winter."[9] Around 870 the island is settled by Ingolf, a Norwegian, at the modern site of Reykjavik.[10] Modern scholars have supported Ari's dating of Ingolf's settlement by using a variety of methods. Describing some of the recent attempts at dating Iceland's settlement, Rafnsson confirms "ice-core chronology, together with tephrochronology, C14 measurements, and archaeological evidence, corroborates Ari's claim that settlement began in about AD 870."[11]

Ari's account helps provide a variety of factors that led to the discovery and settlement of Iceland. The settlement of Iceland by Ingolf is a result of a feud between Ingolf's blood-brother, Leif, and other Vikings. The settlement terms of the feud caused Ingolf and Leif to give up all their possessions, forcing Ingolf to try rebuilding his life. His solution was moving to unsettled Iceland where he and his family had the opportunity to create a new life. Ingolf then was in control of who settled in Iceland, with the immigrants following him needing Ingolf's permission to settle. Ingolf's situation is an example of one reason people moved to Iceland—by last resort when there is nothing left. This was the beginning of the *landnám* that lasted about sixty years and included between ten and twenty thousand people.[12]

Men were not the only ones who claimed land during the *landnám*, as the sagas highlight a number of women who settled the new land. In some instances, women are mentioned because they are the mothers of important children or they are the connection between prominent people. However, in his *Landnámabók* Ari identifies Aud the Deep-Minded as one of the great settlers of the western quarter.[13] She has two chapters devoted to her and several other chapters describing who she gave land to. Through some genealogical work Aud is identified as an ancestor to Ari, which may be part of the reason she is mentioned so often in *Landnámabók*.[14] Aud also shows up in a variety of other sources, including *Saga of the People of Laxardal*, which does help support Ari's view of Aud as an exceptional person and a great settler.

Aud is one of the daughters of Ketil Flatnose, whose own journey is described below. Having fled Norway with her family, Aud arrives first in Scotland, where a short feud soon caused the death of one of her sons. Plotting her escape from Scotland, Aud "had a knorr built secretly in the forest. When it was finished, she made the ship ready and set out with substantial wealth. She took along all her kinsmen who were still alive."[15] From Scotland she settled her family in the Orkney's, marrying off a granddaughter to the Earls of Orkney, and then again relocated to the Faroe Islands before deciding to settle permanently in Iceland. Upon arrival in Iceland, her first brother offers to house only half her party, and Aud instead goes to her other brother who welcomes her entire group warmly. Aud and her followers claim land and supposedly named a number of places and features. After she accrues even more wealth in Iceland, Aud gave more land away to traveling companions and even frees several slaves.[16] The story of Aud not only serves as a heroic journey but also signifies the acceptance of women in leadership roles.

Another interesting passage describing the settlement of Iceland by a woman is the story of Asgerd and her brother Thorolf. Asgerd's husband was killed by King Harald's men, but Asgerd continued with their plan of moving to Iceland. *Landnámabók* records that "Asgerd went to Iceland with their children and her illegitimate brother, Thorolf. She took possession of land. . . . With Asgerd's approval, her brother Thorolf took possession of land west of Fljot."[17] As in the case of Aud, Asgerd is the primary settler because Ari uses the phrase "she took possession." Both women portion land out and are responsible for giving it to others. Ari specifically includes that Thorolf could only claim land "with Asgerd's approval." What becomes clear through these passages is the ability of women to claim and own land, including to divide it up as they see fit, and that it was socially acceptable to do so. If women as settlers or landowners was an unacceptable idea, Ari would not have connected himself with them.

The settlers that follow throughout the *landnám* period, which ended by 930, had a variety of reasons for settling. As Fitzhugh describes, a variety of theories and ideas abound for why people settled the North Atlantic islands during the Viking Age. "Developments in ship construction and seafaring skills; internal stress from population growth and scarce land; loss of personal freedom as political and economic centralization progressed; and the rise of state-sponsored Christianity over pagan belief have all been cited."[18] While no one theory is the only explanation nor incorrect, each factor played a role in forcing people out of their homes in Norway and elsewhere and into the North Atlantic.

A major factor pushing people out of Scandinavia and into Iceland and later Greenland was the development of political and economic centralization. Rafnsson concludes that "one of the most important reasons for the settlement of Iceland was the tyranny of the Norwegian king."[19] As the Vikings continued to gain riches, wealth, and fame from exploits around continental Europe and the British Isles, Viking chieftains consolidated power and began creating small kingdoms on the Medieval European model. Norway, Sweden, and Denmark started to form kings and courts as states began to grow. This altered the power structure in the Scandinavian lands. People who were once independent now had a powerful lord whom they were supposed to be subservient to. This was less evident for the poor farmer, but more noticeable for the rich chieftains.

Egil's Saga illustrates the way King Harald Fairhair gained power and centralized his authority while creating problems for the chieftains who used to be independent. Solvi Chopper, the son of slain chieftain and minor-king Hunthjof, warns another king of what will happen as King Harald moves to take his land:

> It will not be very long before the same happens to you, because I think Harald will be here soon, once he has brought slavery and suffering to everyone he chooses in North More and Romsdal. You will face the same choice we had: either to defend your property and freedom by staking all the men you can hope to muster—and I will provide my forces too against such aggression and injustice—or to follow the course taken by the people of Naumdal who voluntarily entered servitude and became Harald's slaves. My father felt it an honour to die nobly as king of his own realm rather than become subservient to another king in his old age. I think you will feel the same, and so will any other stalwarts who want to prove their worth.[20]

According to this passage in *Egil's Saga*, the local chieftains and petty kings find it better to die than to be subservient to a large, powerful king. After the ensuing battle and King Harald's victory, the saga relays that "many people fled the country to escape this tyranny and settled various uninhabited parts of many places."[21]

The Saga of the People of Laxardal offers another example of the power grab that was going on during the *landnám* time and how that forced a powerful family to move away from Norway. The saga introduces Ketil Flatnose as a "powerful hersir in Norway and came from a prominent family."[22] Shortly thereafter the saga tells us that:

> During Ketil's later years King Harald Fairhair grew so powerful that no petty king or other man of rank could thrive in Norway unless he had received his title from the king.... Ketil learned that the king had intended to offer him the same terms as others, namely to submit to his authority without receiving any compensation for kinsmen who had been killed by the king's forces.[23]

In response, Ketil and his family make the decision to travel west. Ketil ends in the Hebrides while his sons Helgi Bjolan and Bjorn Ketilsson settled in Iceland.[24]

Using these two sagas as a guide it is easy to see why Norwegians would venture to Iceland. The options of wealthy but less-powerful chieftains and kings against a formidable and powerful king attempting to control all of Norway and consolidate authority, such as Harald Fairhair, were to fight, submit, or flee. As described in the passage from *Egil's Saga* the option to submit to Harald was considered dishonorable, whereas the option to fight was quite honorable. Ketil Flat-nose's dealings with Harald in *The Saga of the People of Laxardal* evidently comes towards the end of Harald's consolidation of power, as it appears well known what will happen to Ketil and his family if they do not submit and fighting Harald no longer appears to be an option. Fleeing the country and settling in new lands—the Hebrides and Iceland in this case—does appear to be honorable, at least from the biased vantage point of the Icelandic sagas.

Boulhosa agrees that the authority of King Harald directly resulted in powerful families moving towards Iceland and other islands. In her interpretation of *Egil's Saga*, she writes "the new, centralized kingship which is born with [Harald] disturbs the harmony based upon traditional structures; his reign also provides an explanation for the settlement of Iceland, and it is of crucial importance in *Egil's Saga* because it leads to Egil's family being forced to leave Norway and settling in Iceland."[25] Whether scholars take these two sagas as absolutely accurate in all details or not, the fact that the king's power was feared and powerful people did not want to submit to his authority but instead chose to emigrate was believable and relatable to the initial saga audiences.

Norway's emigrants chose to go to Iceland because it offered the chance to rebuild a society they desired. Keller describes the change best as he writes that "in Norway, a major political change was brought about by the transition towards a kingdom and state. By emigration, the old social order could be maintained in a new country."[26] It was not only Norwegians who were leaving and looking for new lands in which to create an ideal society, and Norway was not the only country that had these changes in power happening. This was "part of fundamental changes in political and social structure that were taking place in northern Europe when the growth of markets and consolidation of power by kings and courts stimulated the colonization of new lands."[27] The people leaving their homelands did not settle in other established countries because they likely would be subject to the same type of rule and tyranny they had tried to escape. Instead the emigrants settled in Iceland because Iceland had no kings and nobody centralizing power yet.

The saga evidence also concludes that the people settling Iceland were wealthy farmers. "The interpretation of the emigration as essentially aristocratic is supported by twelfth-century evidence that it was the shipowners who commanded the loyalty of numerous followers. It is therefore a reasonable assumption that chieftains and rich merchant farmers organized the settlement of the Faeroes, Iceland, and Greenland."[28] It should be noted that the chieftains and wealthy farmers that settled Iceland did not lead the settlement of Iceland, they too came as independent settlers along with other free farmers.[29]

From the time of *landnám* until Iceland's treaty with Norway in 1262, the Norwegian kings tried conquering or controlling Iceland. Norway was undergoing state formation by the thirteenth century, which included multiple attempts at controlling Iceland and Greenland. Norway was their most important trade partner, and many Icelanders and Greenlanders could trace their heritage back to Norway. Influential to Norway's desire to control all of the North Atlantic was the ability to control exotic exports of walrus skin, narwhal tusk, and polar bears, and the extra tax revenue that was possible.[30] Even beyond the profits to be made, however, was the desire of Norway's King Hákon Hákonarson to "be a monarch in the western fashion and to resemble his German, French, and English counterparts."[31] Trying to resemble other European kings meant King Hákon needed more land, as "territorial expansion was the aim of the greatest European monarchies in the thirteenth centuries."[32] The small and independent countries of Iceland and Greenland were ideal targets.

Ari's story of Uni the Dane is an example of King Harald's attempt at conquering Iceland during the time of initial settlement. According to Ari, "Uni, son of Gardar who discovered Iceland, went to Iceland at the suggestion of King Harald [Fairhair] with the intention of conquering the land. The king had promised to make him his earl. . . . When people realised what he wanted, they grew hostile and wouldn't sell him livestock and other necessities, so he wasn't able to stay there."[33] In Ari's story Uni gets sidetracked from his goal of conquest by getting involved in a feud situation over a lover and eventually is killed along with all the people who were supposed to help him conquer Iceland. Norway's king and court constantly play a role in the different sagas and the survival of Iceland.

Another major cause for the migration from Scandinavian lands to Iceland was the need for land, especially because "there were no activities more central to Norse identity than farming."[34] The reports given by early discoverers Gardar and Floki told of vast amounts of woodlands and great quantities of fish, which were all some people needed to hear in order to support their decisions to leave their homelands. As the population across Scandinavia increased and the amount of useable land decreased, uninhabitable land had to have been appealing. This was especially true of people who had been living in the crowded mountainous region of western Norway.[35] Fitzhugh describes the scene as beginning "with a rush of optimism: they saw the opportunity to obtain new lands, wild game, livestock herds, and becomes lords of the local manor."[36]

The opportunity to farm was essential to the lifestyle of the Norse settlers, and another one of the reasons why so many settlers were drawn to Iceland as opposed to well established countries throughout Europe. Iceland's "extensive coastal plains and inland valleys, remote from the sea"[37] offered ample space for settlers to create farms. Kaland describes the role of farms as a vital aspect of being able to survive in the North Atlantic as she describes their expansion. "As the Vikings expanded their domain between AD 800 and 1050, it was animal husbandry that was the basis for their economy and made possible their colonization of the North Atlantic islands, of Greenland, and, for a brief period, northeastern North America."[38] It should also be pointed out that "most Vikings ate food produced on farms, supplemented with fish from the sea, lakes, and streams. Sea and land mammals were caught and eaten in all areas where they were accessible."[39] The descriptions given by Gardar and Floki, as well as other travelers to Iceland, depicted Iceland as an ideal spot for any Viking or Norse settler to make a home, with all the necessities they needed to replicate their homelands.

The settlers brought with them a variety of livestock that they needed in order to survive. In their Scandinavian homelands, the farms would have been small, as Fitzhugh describes that "most farms occupied only a few thousand square feet of in-field pasture in which they grazed cows, horses, sheep, and goats, and if they were lucky, a small number of pigs."[40] Vésteinsson notes that once arriving in Iceland, however, "Iceland would have seemed a prosperous land, with plenty of fish and seal, good and extensive meadows to provide fodder, and enormous tracts of pasture."[41] Early settlers were able to claim extensive amounts of land, sometimes even entire fjords. In *Landnámabók*, for example, Helgi the Lean claimed all of Eyjafjord in northern Iceland,[42] which stretches inland approximately 60 km and is up to 25 km wide.[43] The vast tracts of land available to early settlers made Iceland so appealing to the Scandinavians living in overcrowded areas with little land opportunities.

If large areas of suitable farm land was a predominant pull factor, the wide variety of large game was a strong second factor. Rafnsson points out the opportunity to hunt walrus in Iceland by identifying Rosmhvalanes as a major peninsula that translates to "walrus peninsula."[44] He also notes "remains of great auks have been found in excavations in southwestern Iceland, for example in Reykjavik. It is now extinct but could be found in Iceland, Greenland, and Newfoundland until recently."[45] Both of these animals could be utilized for food as well as a source of valuable items. *Egil's Saga* tells how the chieftain Skallagrim utilized the natural resources after he first settled there:

> [Skallagrim] had a farmstead built on Alftanes and ran another farm there, and rowed out from it to catch fish and cull seals and gather eggs, all of which were there in great abundance. There was plenty of driftwood to take back to his farm. Whales beached, too, in great numbers, and there was wildlife for the taking at this hunting post; the animals were not used to men and would never flee. . . . The islands offshore were called Hvalseyjar (Whale islands), because whales congregated there. Skallagrim also sent his men upriver to catch salmon.[46]

A resourceful settler like Skallagrim could be extremely successful and always have plenty of food due to the wide range of resources available to them. Because of Iceland's volcanic origins, most of the wild game came from the water or at least could travel through the water. That also meant there were no large land predators to worry about, such as bears.

Iceland provided a nearly ideal location for Scandinavians who needed an escape and wanted to find a place they could transform into their ideal society. The combination of political changes going on in Europe and the discovery of uninhabited land that offered vast amounts of farmable land and easy access to animals to supplement their diet made Iceland an ideal spot for many people to settle. The settlers also shaped their lives and their interactions with each other based mostly on cooperation and the need to survive. Greenland's settlement begins with very similar goals but is unable to manage the same level of subsistence found in Iceland.

Like Iceland, the majority of Greenland is covered by a massive inland glacier or ice sheet, the second largest in the world behind Antarctica.[47] The ice sheet covers nearly five-sixths of Greenland's surface and is up to 10,000 feet thick. Between the sea and the ice sheet are mountains that reach as high as 12,000 feet, almost resembling a bowl that holds the ice. Greenland covers nearly 850,000 square miles and is the world's largest island, stretching from about 60° North to almost 85° North, and sits almost entirely in the Arctic Circle.[48] The early Norse would have noticed a warmer climate in Greenland than in Iceland, even though Greenland's summers are shorter. Greenland's shorter summers allow for mostly birch and willow in the areas settled by the Norse, although a small charcoal layer around the time of Norse arrival indicates Greenland may have once sustained a small forest, which the Norse burned to make way for farmland.[49]

Greenland's settlement is very similar to the settlement of Iceland. Greenland also had a group of people present before the Norse came. Erik the Red originated in Norway like Ingolf, but unlike Ingolf he was forced to leave because he was convicted of murder. He was then forced out of Iceland for similar charges. Farming is the central aspect of civilization in Greenland, although the size of the farms and the availability of land is not the same in Greenland for its initial *landnám* as compared to Iceland's. The number of settlers in Greenland are approximately one-tenth of the number that originally moved to Iceland. While Iceland offers a wide range of written sources describing the *landnám* period and life in Iceland, very few resources exist regarding Greenland. The major sources are short passages in Ari's histories and two relatively short sagas: *The Greenlander Saga* and *Erik the Red's Saga*. Thankfully a growing number of archaeological work is being done in Greenland to create a more complete picture of life in Norse Greenland.

Before Erik the Red and the Norse arrived in Greenland, the island was home to the late Dorset culture, approximately covering the eighth and ninth centuries. Archaeological evidence shows the Dorset culture ranged along the northwestern and western coasts of Greenland, although the evidence in Disko Bay shows a mixture of both Thule and Dorset cultures around the same time period.[50] *Íslendingabók* describes Erik's discovery of the island and includes discovery of previous settlement: "[Erik the Red and crew] discovered human dwellings both to the east and west of the land, as well as fragments of skin-boats and stone tools, from which it could be conjectured that the same kind of people had traveled there as had settled Vinland: Greenlanders called them Skraelings."[51] The Greenland settlement would not have any other contact with Thule or Dorset cultures in Greenland for nearly two more centuries.

Greenland was first spotted by a European named Gunnbjörn, who much like Naddodd was blown off course. While off course he saw some islands which then were called the Gunnbjörn Skerries.[52] In his account of Hallbjorn, Ari describes the journey of Snæbjorn and his search for the land to the west of Iceland. After leading men into armed conflict with a murder and his friends, Snæbjorn set sail from Iceland for Greenland, and apparently landed somewhere on Greenland. He and some of his crew were murdered by other crewmembers while on Greenland, and the murderers eventually sailed back to Iceland.[53] The way Ari briefly mentions the information about Snæbjorn implies there should be common knowledge of him and his journey—perhaps a saga existed regarding Snæbjorn but was since lost. Despite the murder of Snæbjorn, the stories about the Gunnbjörn Skerries likely continued to be passed on in Iceland. Erik the Red was the first Scandinavian to explore the land happened upon by Gunnbjörn.

Erik the Red and his father, Thorvald, had to leave Norway "because of killings they were involved in."[54] Eventually, Erik again was involved in issues of murder after his slaves created a landslide that fell on another Icelander's farm. The farmer's kinsman, Eyjolf, retaliated and killed the slaves, which caused Erik to then kill Eyjolf.[55] This series of events led to Erik's sentence of fjörbaugsgarðr, an expulsion of three years from all of Iceland, not just his local district.[56] In 982 he then left Iceland and landed on the west coast of Greenland, setting in motion the settlement and *landnám* of Greenland.

The people who settled Greenland also had their own set of push and pull factors. Similar to the reasons people needed to leave their Scandinavian homelands for Iceland, the Icelanders were beginning to suffer from poor farmland and overcrowding. Another possibility is that Iceland was not so much over-crowded but rather, as some scholars put it, "over-chieftained."[57] Similar to the events in Norway, some chieftains were trying to take too much power or were constantly involved in feuds. As Erik praised the land on his return to Iceland, those in need of escape or in search of land, adventure, and fame joined the settlement party. Buckland describes the mindset of the hopeless farmer and immigrant well when he writes that "to the poor and small farmers of Iceland, which was already close to, or perhaps past, its land capacity for self-sufficient farms, the exploration of Greenland in 984 by Erik the Red provided an opportunity for survival."[58] This is seen in an example from *Erik the Red's Saga* that tells the story of Thorbjorn, who at a wedding feast declares:

> My financial situation, however, which has not up to now been considered an unworthy one, is on the decline. So I would rather leave my farm than live with this loss of honour, and rather leave the country

than shame my family. I intend to take up the offer made to me by my friend Erik the Red.... I intend to head for Greenland this summer.[59]

As the emigrants left Iceland they carried with them their way of life, which was based heavily on farming. Around 985 or 986, Erik led twenty-five ships towards Greenland to make a permanent settlement. Ari relays that only fourteen ships successfully reached Greenland.[60] Ari does not say the fate of the other eleven ships, which must have sunk or returned to Iceland.[61] The colonists then settled two areas, named the Eastern Settlement and the Western Settlement, both made up of a number of small villages or towns scattered across the different fjords.[62]

The Eastern Settlement was by far the larger of the two settlements, and also featured the best available port in Greenland—Herjolfsnes. Two thirds of the farms were located in or around the Eastern Settlement.[63] The name of the settlement is misleading, as it actually lies near the middle or western portion of the extreme southern tip of Greenland, probably near modern day Qaqortoq. The Western Settlement lies about 180 miles north along Greenland's western coastline. The hunting grounds, Norðrsetur, was around the Disko Bay area, over three hundred miles north of the Western Settlement.[64]

Having reaching Greenland, the settlers seemed to be content to settle and not plan on exploring more lands, at least not initially. The *Saga of the Greenlanders* tells of Bjarni, an Icelandic merchant who decided to follow his father to Greenland, seeing three other lands that did not match the description of Greenland he was after, even though two appear inhabitable. These are the mysterious lands later set out for by Erik's son, Leif, and led to the brief settlement of Vinland in North America. Bjarni and his men, despite seeing other suitable lands, eventually find Greenland and settle there.[65]

Like Iceland and Norway, Greenland has an extensive system of fjords and inlets. The best land in Greenland went to Erik the Red and is called Eriksfjord, which contains the site of his farm known as Brattahlid. Norlund describes the attraction of Brattahlid by writing that "no other fjord can compare with Eriksfjord, and the country round Brattahlid where he built his farm is more like Iceland than any other terrain in all Greenland."[66] Farmable land again dictated where the settlers would make their homes. The coastal area of Greenland was avoided by most settlers because much of the usable farmland was inside the fjords. The climate inside some of Greenland's fjords was also comparable or better than the climate in parts of Iceland. Buckland notes the fjords' attraction for the early settlers and the speed they were chosen, suggesting "all available sites for farms in both the Eastern and Western Settlement of Greenland were rapidly occupied, and even the inner fjords of Greenland with their warmer, if shorter, summers would have seemed preferable to the more maritime areas of Iceland."[67] A recent survey of the sites in

Greenland's Eastern Settlement, the larger of the two, approximates there were 250 permanent farms and 80 minor farms through the settlement's existence.[68]

The Greenland settlers had hope for creating a better version of the lives they had left in Iceland, just like Iceland's early settlers had hoped. Their society and the settlement pattern show the importance the Norse placed on animal husbandry.[69] Olafsson connects Iceland's lifestyle with Greenland's settlement when he writes "the population that moved from Iceland to Greenland in around the year 1000 attempted to maintain the lifestyle they had known in Iceland, keeping herds of sheep and cows and even horses. The extreme climatic conditions in Greeland, however, were very different from those in Iceland."[70] Keller agrees and suggests that because of the way "most of the ruin-groups feature barns, byres and pens, it can hardly be doubted that animal husbandry was the most important element in the Norse Greenland economy. The herding economy has also been considered the most vulnerable element of their culture."[71] Recent research has suggested that even the sites that would be less attractive to the Norse were claimed and settled during Greenland's *landnám* period.[72]

One problem with animal husbandry as the staple of their economy and lifestyle is the need to feed the animals, especially throughout winter. Norlund estimates that a cow requires twelve and half kilos of hay per day to survive when not grazing in a field. He then estimated two hundred days as the minimum number of days a cow would be penned in, which totals 2,500 kilos of hay to sustain one cow. Norlund also estimates a horse would need to pull twenty five loads of hay to ensure one cow could survive the winter. The average number of cows on a medium Greenland farm ranged from ten to twenty. Therefore, at the minimum, the farmer of a medium sized farm needed to store 25,000 kilos of hay if he wanted his cows to survive the winter. That means the farmer needed to manage 250 horse loads during a short growing season — approximately 150 days from start to finish — simply for ten heads of cattle.[73] It is understandable why Keller and other scholars refer to this type of lifestyle as "vulnerable."

Much to the settlers' benefit, Greenland had a wide range of large game animals to be hunted or caught — more than Iceland offered. Archaeological evidence identifies "seal meat was eaten more than any other kind of flesh."[74] The harp seal seems to be present the most, at least in areas that had easy access to the coast. The inland farms, however, used caribou as a primary meat source.[75] Gad points out the peculiarity that "the middens contain few remains of domestic animals, whereas there are quite substantial remains of game, such as reindeer, various seal species, walrus, very few bears, astonishingly few Arctic foxes, a considerable number of polar hares, and remains of the various big whale species, among them the right whale."[76] This evidence implies that the Greenlanders were able to sustain themselves—at least in the early part of the settlement—on food that was caught or hunted and did not rely heavily on raising domestic animals to eat. Another abundant food source is the cod found near Greenland's coast.

One of the most fascinating sources for understanding how a typical Greenland farm was set up is found at the site called "Farm Beneath the Sand." It was discovered in 1990 and benefited from modern archaeological techniques, and has provided a wealth of knowledge as it appears the farm was in use during nearly the entire period of Norse colonization in Greenland. The farm provides evidence of domesticated animals throughout the life of the farm, dating back to the *landnám* period, in the form of bone remains, waste, and even some hoof prints.[77] These animals remains include "cattle, horses, sheep, and goats. The proportions of each kind of bones show that the stock was mostly sheep or goats and to a lesser extent cows and horses."[78] The evidence also suggests that the farmer tried to fertilize the field with animal waste, the first find of its kind in Norse settlements.[79]

The farm also reveals the typical types of hunted animals, as Berglund reports that "most bones came from such game as hare, seal, and caribou, confirming that the domestic animals were kept for milk and wool."[80] The bones of larger game were rare, such as polar bears, arctic wolves, and walrus. Whale bones were also found, mostly vertebra, although the suggestion is they were the result of beached whales and not from intentionally hunting them.[81] This fits with the idea that the Norse settler relied heavily on farming for food and raising domesticated animals, and hunting animals was a secondary food source instead of a primary food source.

Most intriguing about this farm is the insight it offers about the residents. The evidence says the residents were Roman Catholic, at some point people named Thor, Bardur, and Bjork were connected to the farm, and children were raised there. Berglund relays that "finds of toys such as a miniature shoemaker's last and wooden model knives reveal that play was part of their life and that simulation of grown-up life was, then as now, an important part of children's play."[82] As research into the farm and its contents continue, more will be learned as to how the farm developed and the farmers changed and survived in Norse Greenland.

While the written evidence is sparse regarding Greenland's settlement, a fairly clear picture has emerged. Greenland was settled as an escape for people who either struggled to make a life in Iceland or were forced to leave for political or social reasons. Creating sustainable farms on what they hoped would be quality land was the primary purpose of the *landnám*. Even though Greenland offered more hunting opportunities than Iceland, the primary food supply and means of existence revolved around the farm.

The settlement and *landnám* periods of both Iceland and Greenland have some striking similarities, as well as their differences. Both Iceland and Greenland saw the remnants of previous peoples, but the Norse did not have to actually interact with the previous residents of the islands. While virtually no scholarship exists on this topic, potential contact could drastically change the approach to settlement and the way of life. The *papar* in Iceland likely had little to offer, but an observation by Erik the Red of the Dorset people that left behind skin boats would have demonstrated the importance of utilizing the sea for a primary food source. Beyond that, the settlers had no other peoples to contend with for land or resources in either place. Ingolf and Erik were both able to pick the land they settled and could help determine who else would settle land near them. This provided them the opportunity to create stronger bonds by rewarding people with quality land they parceled out from their own land and surrounding their own farms with other reliable or successful farms.

All the settlers to Iceland and Greenland also shared the common goal, perhaps romanticized, of creating the ideal society that was no longer available to them in their homelands. Political and social issues were a driving factor out of Norway under King Harald Fairhair, and the attempts of local chieftains to gain power in Iceland helped force people towards new, uninhabited lands. The *landnám* was an independent movement in both Iceland and Greenland, and settlers could claim land as they saw fit. Neither settlement was directed by a king or even a powerful chieftain, although Ingolf and Erik likely had considerable influence over early settlers.

The great dependence on farming and animal husbandry is overwhelming in both Iceland and Greenland. The farming techniques used in Norway carried over into Iceland and then into Greenland. The settlers of both lands were drawn in by the appeal of getting much more acreage for their farms than they had in overcrowded Norway, but that also meant more animals to maintain and care for. While both colonies fought the battle for subsistence, Greenland actually had a wider variety of other resources available to them, including the seemingly endless hunting ground known as *Norðrsetur*.[83] Based on a strong abundance of resources, both colonies should have been successful.

Many aspects of the early settlements in Iceland and Greenland are similar. The two colonies, though beginning a century apart, continued to grow and thrive in the North Atlantic. From this point on many aspects about the growth and development of Greenland and Iceland are similar. The size of the colonies, with Iceland having nearly ten times as many people as Greenland at the end of their respective *landnám* periods, impacted the way the societies developed. Now that their settlements are better understood, the growth and development of Icelandic and Greenlandic societies can be explained and understood.

NOTES

1. Jesse L Byock, *Medieval Iceland: Society, Sagas, and Power* (Berkeley: University of California Press, 1988), 26–28.
2. William P. Patterson et al., "Two Millennia of North Atlantic Seasonality and Implications for Norse Colonies," *Proceedings of the National Academy of Sciences of the United States of America* 107, no. 12 (March 23, 2010): 5309.
3. The original *Landnámabók* has been lost, but the version utilized here is a translation of Sturla Thordarson's version of *Landnámabók* finished around 1280, commonly referred to as Sturlubók.
4. Ari Thorgilsson, *Landnámabók: The Book of Settlements*, trans. Paul Edwards and Hermann Pálsson (Winnipeg, Man.: University of Manitoba Press, 2006), 16.
5. Ibid., 15.
6. Dicuil, "Liber de Mensura Orbis Terrae," in *The Viking Age: A Reader*, ed. Angus A. Somerville and R. Andrew McDonald, trans. J.J. Tierney (Toronto: University of Toronto Press, 2010), 330.
7. Thorgilsson, *Landnámabók: The Book of Settlements*, 16.
8. Ibid., 17.
9. Ibid., 18.
10. Else Roesdahl, *The Vikings* (New York: Penguin Books, 1998), 268.
11. Sveinbjorn Rafnsson, "The Atlantic Islands," in *The Oxford Illustrated History of the Vikings*, ed. Peter Sawyer (Oxford: Oxford University Press, 2001), 122.
12. Jesse L Byock, *Viking Age Iceland* (New York: Penguin Books, 2001), 9.
13. Thorgilsson, *Landnámabók: The Book of Settlements*, 80.
14. Judith Jesch, *Women in the Viking Age* (Woodbridge, Suffolk: Boydell Press, 1991), 80.
15. Keneva Kunz, trans., "The Saga of the People of Laxardal," in *The Sagas of Icelanders: A Selection* (New York: Penguin Books, 2001), 278.
16. Ibid., 279–280.
17. Thorgilsson, *Landnámabók: The Book of Settlements*, 129.
18. William W Fitzhugh, "Puffins, Ringed Pins, and Runestones: The Viking Passage to America," in *Vikings: The North Atlantic Saga*, ed. William W Fitzhugh and Elizabeth I Ward (Washington, D.C.: Smithsonian Institution Press, in association with the National Museum of Natural History, 2000), 17.
19. Rafnsson, "The Atlantic Islands," 118–119.
20. Bernard Scudder, trans., "Egil's Sagas," in *The Sagas of Icelanders: A Selection* (New York: Penguin Books, 2001), 10.
21. Ibid., 11–12.
22. Kunz, "The Saga of the People of Laxardal," 276.
23. Ibid.
24. Thorgilsson, *Landnámabók: The Book of Settlements*, 23; Kunz, "The Saga of the People of Laxardal," 277–278.
25. Patricia Pires Boulhosa, *Icelanders and the Kings of Norway: Mediaeval Sagas and Legal Texts* (Leiden: Brill Academic Pub, 2005), 166.
26. Christian Keller, "Vikings in the West Atlantic: A Model of Norse Greenlandic Medieval Society," in *The North Atlantic Frontier of Medieval Europe: Vikings and Celts*, ed. James Muldoon, vol. 3, The Expansion of Latin Europe, 1000-1500 (Surrey, England: Ashgate Publishing Limited, 2009), 27.
27. Haraldur Olafsson, "Sagas of Western Expansion," in *Vikings: The North Atlantic Saga*, ed. William W Fitzhugh and Elizabeth I Ward (Washington, D.C.: Smithsonian Institution Press, in association with the National Museum of Natural History, 2000), 144.
28. Rafnsson, "The Atlantic Islands," 118.
29. Byock, *Viking Age Iceland*, 8.
30. David Bregaint, "Conquering Minds: Konungs Skuggsia and the Annexation of Iceland in the Thirteenth Century," *Scandinavian Studies* 84, no. 4 (2012): 442.

31. Ibid., 442–443.
32. Ibid., 443.
33. Thorgilsson, *Landnámabók: The Book of Settlements*, 114.
34. Fitzhugh, "Puffins, Ringed Pins, and Runestones: The Viking Passage to America," 14.
35. Olafsson, "Sagas of Western Expansion," 144.
36. Fitzhugh, "Puffins, Ringed Pins, and Runestones: The Viking Passage to America," 19.
37. Paul C Buckland, "The North Atlantic Environment," in *Vikings: The North Atlantic Saga*, ed. William W Fitzhugh and Elizabeth I Ward (Washington, D.C.: Smithsonian Institution Press, in association with the National Museum of Natural History, 2000), 147.
38. Sigrid H.H. Kaland and Irmelin Martens, "Farming and Daily Life," in *Vikings: The North Atlantic Saga*, ed. William W Fitzhugh and Elizabeth I Ward (Washington, D.C.: Smithsonian Institution Press, in association with the National Museum of Natural History, 2000), 42.
39. Ibid., 44.
40. Fitzhugh, "Puffins, Ringed Pins, and Runestones: The Viking Passage to America," 14.
41. Orri Vésteinsson, "The Archaeology of Landnam: Early Settlement in Iceland," in *Vikings: The North Atlantic Saga*, ed. William W Fitzhugh and Elizabeth I Ward (Washington, D.C.: Smithsonian Institution Press, in association with the National Museum of Natural History, 2000), 165.
42. Thorgilsson, *Landnámabók: The Book of Settlements*, 97.
43. "Earth Snapshot - Eyjafjörður, Central Northern Iceland's Longest Fjord," accessed December 29, 2014, http://www.eosnap.com/snapshots/eyjafjor%C3%B0ur-central-northern-icelands-longest-fjord/.
44. Rafnsson, "The Atlantic Islands," 119.
45. Ibid., 120.
46. Scudder, "Egil's Sagas," 48.
47. M. Tedesco et al., "Arctic Report Card—Greenland Ice Sheet," *Arctic Report Card*, January 27, 2015, http://www.arctic.noaa.gov/reportcard/greenland_ice_sheet.html.
48. Eske Brun, "Greenland," *Arctic* 19, no. 1 (March 1, 1966): 62.
49. Buckland, "The North Atlantic Environment," 148.
50. Finn Gad, *History of Greenland: I. Earliest Times to 1700*, trans. Ernst Dupont, First Canadian edition (McGill-Queen's University Press, 1971), 18.
51. Ari Thorgilsson, "Íslendingabók," in *The Viking Age: A Reader*, ed. Angus A. Somerville and R. Andrew McDonald (Toronto: University of Toronto Press, 2010), 346.
52. Gad, *History of Greenland*, 27.
53. Thorgilsson, *Landnámabók: The Book of Settlements*, 73.
54. Ibid., 48.
55. Ibid., 48–49.
56. Gad, *History of Greenland*, 29.
57. Andrew J. Dugmore, Christian Keller, and Thomas H. McGovern, "Norse Greenland Settlement: Reflections on Climate Change, Trade, and the Contrasting Fates of Human Settlements in the North Atlantic Islands," *Arctic Anthropology* 44, no. 1 (January 1, 2007): 16.
58. Buckland, "The North Atlantic Environment," 148.
59. Keneva Kunz, trans., "Eirik the Red's Saga," in *The Sagas of Icelanders: A Selection* (New York: Penguin Books, 2001), 657.
60. Thorgilsson, *Landnámabók: The Book of Settlements*, 49.
61. Poul Norlund, *Viking Settlers in Greenland and Their Descendants during Five Hundred Years* (New York: Kraus Reprint Co., 1971), 19–20.

62. Keller, "Vikings in the West Atlantic: A Model of Norse Greenlandic Medieval Society," 25.
63. Norlund, *Viking Settlers in Greenland and Their Descendants during Five Hundred Years*, 22–23.
64. Ibid., 95.
65. Keneva Kunz, trans., "The Saga of the Greenlanders," in *The Sagas of Icelanders: A Selection* (New York: Penguin Books, 2001), 636–52.
66. Norlund, *Viking Settlers in Greenland and Their Descendants during Five Hundred Years*, 21.
67. Buckland, "The North Atlantic Environment," 148.
68. Orri Vésteinsson, "Parishes and Communities in Norse Greenland," *Journal of the North Atlantic* 2, no. sp2 (January 1, 2009): 144, doi:10.3721/037.002.s215.
69. Jette Arneborg, "Norse Greenland: Reflections on Settlement and Depopulation," in *Contact, Continuity, and Collapse: The Norse Colonization of the North Atlantic*, ed. James H Barrett (Turnhout, Belgium: Brepols, 2003), 166.
70. Olafsson, "Sagas of Western Expansion," 145.
71. Keller, "Vikings in the West Atlantic: A Model of Norse Greenlandic Medieval Society," 34.
72. Arneborg, "Norse Greenland: Reflections on Settlement and Depopulation," 168.
73. Norlund, *Viking Settlers in Greenland and Their Descendants during Five Hundred Years*, 68–69.
74. Ibid., 64.
75. Ibid.
76. Gad, *History of Greenland*, 39.
77. Joel Berglund, "The Farm Beneath the Sand," in *Vikings: The North Atlantic Saga*, ed. William W Fitzhugh and Elizabeth I Ward (Washington, D.C.: Smithsonian Institution Press, in association with the National Museum of Natural History, 2000), 298.
78. Ibid.
79. Ibid.
80. Ibid., 299.
81. Ibid.
82. Ibid., 302.
83. Gad, *History of Greenland*, 86.

THREE
Changes in Society and Religion

Greenland attempted to mimic the social structures of Iceland but failed to do so completely. The power structures were the same in both colonies, but the power in Greenland rarely shifted hands whereas the power in Iceland was very fluid and constantly shifting. A major problem for replicating Icelandic society in Greenland was Greenland's small population and a lower economic base. Another major change in the social structure revolved around the conversion to Christianity, which happened independently in both colonies.

Comparing the social structures between Iceland and Greenland also requires understanding the way the structures and organization changed. The changes that took place in each society explain analyses that at first appear to be contradicting. Keller, for example, says that "the society in Greenland had much in common with that of Iceland during the so-called 'Freestate' or 'Commonwealth' Period."[1] Olafsson, on the other hand, claims that "only in the core settlement of Brattahlid-Gardar, where the bishop lived, was there a sense of community and social organization like that which existed in Iceland."[2] Both statements are accurate because Keller references the first half of the settlement's existence, before the power in Greenland began to be consolidated around the bishop while the power in Iceland was in the hands of a number of chieftains. The changes in Greenland also forced farmers to spend more time working their fields and tending to the livestock in order to survive, making them less inclined to get overly involved in different issues or even spend much time traveling into the populated areas.

The immigrants to Iceland and Greenland had left their homes for uninhabited lands in order to create their ideal lifestyles. As described earlier, much of that revolved around farming larger pieces of land than were available at home. One of the push factors was the tyranny and the power of those in charge, most notably King Harald Fairhair. Because of the changes implemented by the state-forming Scandinavian kings, the Icelanders and the Greenlanders saw themselves as "keepers of the ancient Norwegian individual freedom."[3] Many of the sagas offer examples of the relationships between kings and Icelanders, and their apathetic approach towards the king. In *The Saga of the People of Laxardal* an Icelander, Hoskuld, sails for Norway. "They set out to sea, had favourable winds and made land in the south of Norway, in Hordaland, where the trading town of Bergen was later established. He had the ship drawn ashore there, as important kinsmen of his lived nearby, although they are not mentioned by name. King Hakon was then in Vik. Hoskuld did not proceed on to the king, as his kinsmen received him with open arms."[4] Instead of following tradition and greeting the king, Hoskuld skipped meeting the king which was taken as a mild insult.

Another example from the same saga gives another look at the Icelander's arrogance towards a Norwegian king, this time King Olaf. Thorkel Eyjolfsson was staying in Norway and was found measuring the king's church early one morning. The conversation between Thorkel and King Olaf began: "The king went over to him immediately and said, 'What are you up to, Thorkel? Do you plan to cut timber for your church in Iceland on this model?' Thorkel answered, 'Right you are, my lord.'"[5] The conversation continued when Olaf mockingly suggested that cutting two ells off each beam would still allow Thorkel to build the largest church in Iceland. In his rejection of Olaf's suggestion, Thorkel tells the king he could do without his timber and can manage on his own.

> The king then said, in a pacifying tone, "You are a man of great worth, and of no small ambition. Of course it's absurd for a farmer's son to compete with us. But it is not true that I begrudge you the timber. If you should manage to build a church with it, it will never be so large as to contain your own conceit. But unless I am mistaken, people will have little use of this timber, and even less so will you be able to build any structure with it." With that their conversation came to an end. The king walked away and it was clear that he disliked Thorkel's disregard for his advice.[6]

Thorkel, partly from pride and partly from disregard for the king's status, believes he and his men in Iceland are able to complete a building project equally as large as one the king had done, despite the fact they had no king.

Although the Icelanders and Greenlanders disliked the concept of a king and centralized authority, both settlements did have "elements of statehood: a national legislature and a well-defined legal system that embraced the entire country."[7] This system was based on relationships between chieftains (*goði* or *goðar*, pl.) and the free farmers (*bóndi* or *bændr*, pl.). The *goðar* relied on the *bændr* for support at the assemblies, or

Things, while the *bændr* relied on the *goðar* for help, advocacy, and to settle disputes.[8] It has been determined that not all chieftains necessarily had control over men, while the term *goðar* implies they had at least some followers, and some *goðar* also had religious roles before the conversion to Christainity.[9] Outside the Church hierarchy and unlike the rest of medieval Europe, the only titles that existed in Iceland were the Lawspeaker and the *goði*.[10]

Different than the feudal and manorial systems, the *bændr* were never bound to any particular *goði* and apparently had the option to change their allegiances as they saw fit.[11] The *bændr* could, at least in theory, choose from nearly fifty to sixty different *goðar* at any one time.[12] Sigurðsson describes the consequences of an ineffective chieftain as when "the chieftain failed to manage his cheiftancy satisfactorily, it could prompt farmers to move away for their own safety. There was a high level of mobility in society, and farmers went in search of more powerful, stronger chieftains who could protect them and their interests."[13] The *goðar*, therefore, had to have either the skills or the wealth to draw people to their side and maintain those relationships. The description of Gizurr Thorvaldsson reveals several important traits of a chieftain:

> Gizzur Thorvaldsson . . . became a powerful chieftain, and an intelligent and popular man . . . Gizurr was of moderate height, a very accomplished man, with good limbs and keen-eyed—he had piercing eyes, intelligent in expression; he was better spoken than most men in this country, affable, with a very strong voice; not an impetuous man but one whose advice was always highly valued. And yet it often happened that when he was watching conflicts involving chieftains or his kinsmen, he was rather indifferent about the issue, even uncertain whom he would support. He was rich in kinsmen, and many of the best farmers from the southern district and elsewhere were his friends.[14]

Gizurr evidently was renowned for his physical appearance as much as for his intelligence as well as calm demeanor. As a *goði* he had a large following of *bændr*, which Gizurr treated as friends in order to retain them. Because Gizurr was not guaranteed followers by his position, he had to act justly and politically to maintain or gain followers.

Many of the descriptions of *goðar* include the way their eyes appear. Sigurðsson suggests this is because "hair and eyes symbolized power and noble birth. Other parts of the face, and the face as a whole, were of less interest, but occasionally a chieftain's build, physical attributes and charisma are described."[15] This matches part of the description of Gizurr, and the description of many other *goðar* mentioned throughout the sagas. Ultimately the mental attributes and intelligence of the *goðar* made the biggest difference, while the best *goðar* are often described as charismatic.[16] This makes sense since to succeed as a *goðar* required strong legal and personal skills.

Power transferred between *goðar* based on who had honor and who lost honor. While no special words exist in the Norse language for a social organization based on levels of honor, honor was necessary to one's social standing. The legal historian Miller concludes that "status had to be carefully maintained or aggressively acquired: one's status depended on the condition of one's honor, for it was in the game of honor that rank and reputation was attained and retained. Honor was at stake in virtually every social interaction."[17] As Roesdahl puts the consequences succinctly, "Those who broke the codes lost their honour—their good name—and forfeited their place in society."[18] These interactions included hosting feasts and parties as well as supporting their *bændr* when they needed help, especially through the legal channels at the Things.

The Things, or assemblies, were held on a regular basis in Iceland and Greenland. It is recorded that there were a number of different Things in each quarter of Iceland, but the Althing was the most important because it dealt with issues for the entire island. The Althing was the annual meeting of all *goðar* and brought together hundreds of people every summer.[19] Iceland's Althing traces its roots back to the end of the *landnám* period, marking its creation around 930.[20] The Things, led by the Lawspeaker, had the power to make decisions, settle disputes, and change laws.[21] Any free, adult male could address the crowd or cast a vote at a Thing. The Things' most important function was to maintain peace and order, whether at a local Thing or at the Althing.[22]

Greenland also had a regular Althing. Most historians logically suggest the Althing must have been set up near Erik the Red's farm at Brattahlid, as evidence of booths and fire pits indicative of Thing sites have been found.[23] Once Gardar was assigned as the bishop's home, the Althing permanently relocated there.[24] Their decision to have a bishop was even decided at an Althing meeting. The Althing was still meeting regularly by the end of the fourteenth century as evidenced when the Greenlanders made a law that barred merchants from selling to Greenlanders unless the merchants bought something from them.[25]

The *bændr* and *goðar* had a relationship outside the Thing system as well. The *bændr* relied on the *goðar* especially in situations requiring legal help. *The Saga of Hrafnkel Frey's Godi* offers an example of why one might seek the help of a *goði*, although it also illustrates the dangers associated with feuding. Hrafnkel was a *goði* who killed a shepherd, Einar, who rode on a horse that was Hrafnkel's prized possession. Einar's father, Thorbjorn, rode to the house of another *goði*, Sam, who reluctantly agreed to take up the dispute with Hrafnkel. Sam then publicly declared Hrafnkel responsible for Einar's death, leading to a scene at the Althing. Sam's responsibility is gaining the support of other *goðar* against Hrafnkel. When time to prosecute came, Sam "went boldly up to the court, and immediately began calling forth witnesses, prosecuting his case against Hrafnkel the *Goði* in full accordance with the true law of the land, in a faultless and powerful presentation...Hrafnkel was finally sentenced to greater outlawry at this Thing meeting."[26] Thorbjorn, the slain man's father, was unable to bring a case against Hrafnkel on his own because he was a *bóndi*, therefore needing *goðar* to navigate the laws for him.

While at the Althing, the *goðar* were in charge of the court case and enforcing the results as they so chose. Using the example of Sam and Hrafnkel, Sam had to first manipulate other *goðar* into voting for an outcome he found favorable. Once Sam believed he had enough votes, he needed to publicly try the case against Hrafnel in front of the assembled crowd at the Althing. Thorbjorn had asked Sam to take on the case because he was not only a *bóndi*, but because that was part of the established relationship between *goðar* and *bændr*. Sam accepts because he was supposed to advocate for his followers as part of that relationship.[27]

Greenland had a similar power system, although fewer people were involved because of the smaller population to draw from. The *goðar* system was likely very small, and had almost no religious function because Christianity was adopted so quickly in Greenland. There is also a reference in Ivar Bárðarson's account from the mid fourteenth century that describes "a large farm which is called [Brattahlid] where the Lawman lives at the farmhouse."[28] Since Bárðarson's visit came a century after the submission of Greenland to Norway's authority, his mention of the Lawman demonstrates that the role of Lawspeaker must still have existed for nearly the whole duration of Norse Greenland's existence. The Lawspeaker was in charge of announcing verdicts and laws to the people, and also was in charge of the order at the Althing.[29] After the Greenland Althing was moved near the bishop's farm at Gardar, the Lawspeaker probably continued to be a secular leader.

We know very little about who the *goðar* were in Greenland. It can be assumed that Erik the Red and his descendants likely retained the title of *goði* once they were in Greenland, particularly since the Lawspeaker still resided at Brattahlid three centuries later. Others are more uncertain, although the saga suggests some of the wealthy farmers may have also been *goðar*, or at least had responsibilities and traits similar to those of Icelandic *goðar*. Thorkel, an early settler at Herjolfsnes in Greenland, is described as "the best of farmers. He gave Thorbjorn and all his companions shelter for the winter, treating them generously."[30] He also was the farmer that others turned to for help and guidance. The saga continues that "since Thorkel was the leading farmer there, people felt it was up to him to try to find out when the hard times which had been oppressing them would let up."[31] This is very similar to the earlier description of Gizurr, but without giving Thorkel a title.

A key aspect of the *goðar* and *bændr* relationship throughout the sagas is their role in feuding. Revisiting *The Saga of Hrafnkel Frey's Godi* shows that sometimes a *goði* is called upon to manage a conflict and the resolution can be sought through the courts at the Things or Althing. However, often times in the sagas the conflicts spiral into feuds and revenge killings—even after a resolution has been reached. The conclusion of the story between Sam and Hrafnkel, as one example, finishes violently. Sam tortures the now outlawed Hrafnkel and takes his farm. Eventually, Hrafnkel kills Sam's rich brother Eyvind who had just returned from a journey abroad. Sam attempts to enlist the help of other chieftains, but is unable to convince them to help in his plight against Hrafnkel. While Sam, acting on behalf of Thorbjorn, prosecuted Hrafnkel for the murder of Einar at the beginning of the saga, Hrafnkel then took on Sam and his family as the object of his vengeance.[32] This is acceptable because the two are both *goðar* and it would be below Hrafnkel to feud with a *bóndi*, Thorbjorn.

The feud system in Norse Iceland was a rather refined process. As seen between Sam and Hrafnkel, "feud is something that takes place between people of relatively equal status and resources . . . feud generally did not exist across social strata."[33] As the Icelanders managed conflicts, they had to determine what was worthy of their time, their settlement, and their lives, because their honor was then on the line if they took a case. An important aspect of the entire conflict and feud process is that "a notion of exchange governs the process, a kind of my-turn/your-turn rhythm, with offensive and defensive positions alternating after each confrontation."[34]

The Tale of Thorstein Staff-Struck is another example of how conflict and revenge killings worked in Medieval Iceland. The protagonist, Thorstein, was given a cheap blow to the head by his opposition, Thord, during a horse fight—gaining Thorstein the moniker "Staff-Struck." When Thorstein learned it was not an accident and Thord intentionally hit him, Thorstein killed him. Thorstein was the son of a *bóndi* and Thord was a farmhand for Bjarni, who appears to be a wealthy *goði*.[35] Bjarni hears of Thord's murder and had Thorstein outlawed. Thorstein did not leave and continued to work on his father's farm. Finally Bjarni hears that Thorstein never left and sends two servant to kill Thorstein. The two servants are killed in the ensuing fight with Thorstein. Bjarni, after being goaded into fighting by his wife, challenges Thorstein to combat. After a day of combat, Bjarni offers Thorstein a deal that would end the need for revenge killings, saying "I will consider myself fully compensated for my three farmhands if you will promise me your loyalty."[36]

This tale never refers to the conflict as a feud, but instead is based on the need for compensation. Bjarni needed to be compensated somehow for the deaths of his three farmhands, and the task fell on himself because Thorstein was an excellent fighter. The sentence of outlawry after the killing of Thord was considered adequate to Bjarni, partly due to the fact that both were farmhands and therefore were not worth too much of

Bjarni's time or concern. Because Bjarni was also a local *goði*, however, it was his job to enforce the punishment of outlawry and ensure Thorstein left. Bjarni's wife took Thorstein's refusal to leave as offense to Bjarni's honor, and it was her persuasion which forced Bjarni to seek a revenge killing for his farmhands.

One of the most famous and in-depth depictions of feuding takes place in *Njal's Saga*. Of note in this saga is that the main action is acted out by the men, although the main motivation for the feud and revenge killings comes from the wives. What begins as insults from Gunnar's wife, Hallgerd, towards Njal's wife, Bergthora, ends with six revenge killings, then Njal, Njal's house, and most of Njal's family are burned alive, and the burnings force Njal's son-in-law to kill fifteen of the people responsible for the burning.[37] While that may oversimplify the plot of the saga, the saga offers a wide range of topics to be interpreted.

Near the beginning of the saga, Gunnar seeks Njal's advice and essentially sues at the Althing to get his kinswoman's dowry back, demonstrating the legal options available to people. Gunnar loses, and then plots an odd scheme with Njal in an attempt to get the dowry, again demonstrating the willingness of Icelanders to use force once the Thing system failed them. After Hallgerd and Bergthora exchange insults, Njal and Gunnar end up on opposite sides of a feud. The revenge killings that take up the middle of the saga are extremely well balanced. Two slaves worth twelve ounces of silver were compensated for, then two men worth one hundred ounces of silver were balanced, and finally two men worth two hundred ounces of silver. Each payment between Gunnar and Njal was considered as fully compensated and the patriarchs had hoped to end the feuds there. Their relatives continued the feud, however, which also illustrates the lack of control over relatives and the stubborn nature of the early Icelanders who took problems into their own hands and disregarded the legal agreements.

All three of these sagas identify a major problem facing the Medieval Icelanders: the lack of enforcement for legal decisions. The general assumption was that honor would keep people accountable. Sam had won his prosecution of Hrafnkel and Hrafnkel should have been forced to submit to the punishment. Thorstein was sentenced to outlawry and should have been forced to go. Gunnar should have been forced to accept the idea he was not getting his kinswoman's dowry back and there should have been enforcement when he tried to forcibly take it. In each scenario, the conflict is able to continue growing and expanding, thereby incorporating more people, because the *goðar* had nobody to answer to if they neglected a punishment.

Whether these sagas and descriptions of feuds and revenge are interpreted as entirely truthful—*Njal's Saga* may be too perfectly symmetrical in the feud process—or simply considered as something that could have happened, they create a window into Iceland's early centuries. While social relationships and legal processes and expectations were well defined in early Iceland, the systems of chieftains and feuds caused power to constantly change hands. Icelandic society began to change, however, as the fluidity of power became static in the hands of six powerful families. A major thrust towards changing Iceland's society was the conversion to Christianity and the implementation of Church hierarchy that followed.

Understanding the development of Christianity across Scandinavia constructs a better frame to understand how and why Iceland adopted Christianity so quickly and how that quick adoption altered society. At the beginning of the Viking Age, the Vikings who traveled throughout northern Europe spent most of their time raiding and looting, which soon developed into trading. Those early Viking chieftains had as their goal to "acquire wealth, which might gain [the chieftains] the reputation of being generous chieftains, to whose standards warriors would flock."[38] As the chieftains gained quality warriors, their power would increase. The more ways a Viking chieftain could demonstrate generosity towards his follows, the more people would want to follow him and voyage with him. This generosity was best done through the gift-giving process. The gift did matter, as the "more exclusive the gift, the higher the esteem of the giver, and the more power concentrated in him."[39] The recipient of the gift was expected to be loyal to the chieftain who gave the gift, thereby creating a type of bond—the more luxurious the gift, the stronger the bond.

Scandinavian kings began to take on Christianity as a religion, in part as a political ploy. The kings and chieftains who accepted Christianity utilized baptism as a way to create an indispensable gift and have a spiritual connection—that of godparent and godchild. The political advantage of baptism can be seen through the "many Vikings [who] were baptized abroad, some of them several times, for baptism was often a condition in a political alliance or in a propitious peace treaty, and the ceremony meant some new clothes, a baptismal gift and a baptismal feast."[40] The willingness of some Vikings to be baptized coincides with their pagan roots. Jochens describes the inclusive nature of the pagan Vikings and how "Nordic polytheism inclined Vikings toward tolerance of other religions; when they arrived in Christian countries, they were generally receptive to the local religion."[41] Christianity was therefore familiar to some Vikings and also was more effective at fostering relationships for chieftains than paganism. That also meant that a chieftain or king could offer better gifts than his competitors, and through that build up a stronger force.

The story of Olaf Tryggvason follows that path in Norway. In 994 he was baptized after entering a peace treaty with England's King Ethelred, and Ethelred was Olaf's godfather. Olaf then fought with Earl Hakon Sigurðsson over Norway, who offered his followers the benefits of Norse paganism. Winroth suggests that "thanks to the danegeld [Olaf] had collected in England, he had more wealth to distribute among his warriors, and thanks to his baptism at the hands of King Ethelred, he had a more prestigious religion to offer."[42] After defeating Hakon, Olaf "set out to convert the country by the sword, and used Christianity as an instrument of power politics in his attempt to subdue the people."[43] Olaf Tryggvason was king of Norway when the Icelanders decided to convert to Christianity. He did not succeed in completely converting Norway—that would be completed by King Olaf Haraldsson, also known as St. Olaf, who was also baptized by Ethelred.

Being converted to Christianity made Olaf connected to Ethelred, and in the culture of gift giving and receiving, needed to be loyal to Ethelred. This made King Harald Bluetooth of Denmark take a slightly different approach to Christianity. The evidence says that King Harald was still a pagan when his father, Gorm, died around 958, because Harald buried his father in an elaborate pagan grave complete with a horse and grave goods.[44] At some point in the next decade, Harald converted to Christianity, although the details of his conversion are uncertain.[45]

German chronicler Widukind of Corvey, who wrote during the late 900s, described that Harald Bluetooth was converted to Christianity through the deeds of a missionary named Poppo. According to Widukind, a feast was being held by Harald with pagans and Poppo in attendance. Harald challenged Poppo to prove his faith, and the missionary accepted the challenge. Widukind relayed that Harald "ordered that a great weight of iron be heated in the fire and he commanded that the cleric carry the glowing iron for the sake of his catholic faith. The confessor of Christ grabbed the iron without hesitation and carried it as far as the king determined. He then showed his unhurt hands to everyone, proving the truth of the catholic faith."[46] Harald then acknowledged that the Christian God would be the only one worshiped.

Adam of Bremen, who wrote to help assert the authority of Hamburg-Bremen over the northern countries and kingdoms, gave a different explanation for Harald's conversion. Adam recorded that Unni, the archbishop of Hamburg-Bremen, became a missionary to the Danes. Unni failed to convert King Gorm, but successfully converted his son Harald. Adam wrote that "Unni made [Harald] so faithful to Christ that, although he himself had not yet received the sacrament of baptism, he permitted the public profession of Christianity which his father always hated."[47] Neither Adam nor Widukind's accounts of Harald's conversion can be substantiated, although Adam's history comes with a very evident attempt to maintain control over the Scandinavian churches.

After converting to Christianity, Harald relocated his parents into a Christian burial, built a church, and erected the famous Jelling runestone, which reads "King Harald had this monument made in memory of his father Gorm and in memory of his mother Thyre; that Harald who won for himself all Denmark and Norway, and made the Danes Christian."[48] The wording used on the runestone is quite precise. Harald does not give anybody or any other ruler credit for his conversion, nor was anybody else responsible for Christianizing Denmark. Instead, according to Harald, he was responsible for making Denmark Christian. Harald's conversion on his own deprived any other ruler of claiming responsibility and therefore Harald's loyalty.[49] Harald used Christianity to help defend his kingdom against imperial expansion and to be part of the same religion as major European kings and rulers.

The events surrounding Christianity in Denmark and Norway are vital to understanding Iceland's conversion. Missionaries, including the priest Thangbrand sent by Norway's King Olaf Tryggvason, had already visited Iceland, and evidently a large group of Icelanders had started to be converted to Christianity.[50] This is beyond the early settlers whom Ari identified as Christians. The scene at the Althing in the summer of 1000 was intense according to Ari, with the Christians and pagans on the verge of combat:

> The heathen men crowded together fully armed, and the sides were so close to violence that it was anyone's guess whether a battle would break out. Next day, Gizur and Hjalti went to the Law Rock to present their case, and the story goes that it was astonishing how well they expressed themselves. However, the result was that one man after another named witnesses, and both sides, Christians and heathens, declared themselves not bound by the laws of the others.[51]

The two sides agreed to let Thorgeir the Lawspeaker, a heathen, make the decision. Thorgeir responded that "each side gets something and we all have one law and a single faith. For sure, if we tear up the law, we tear up the country."[52] With that, he declared that Christianity was to be the religion and the law of Iceland.[53] As part of the compromise, he allowed particular pagan practices to continue. Ari records that "from among the old laws were preserved the right to expose infants and the eating of horseflesh. Private sacrifice was still allowed, but there would be a penalty of lesser outlawry if there were any witnesses. A few years later this heathen practice was abolished like the others."[54]

Ari tells part of the story, and relays Thorgeir's decision as an attempt to avoid conflict and keep the country united, but something is likely missing. Knowing that King Olaf had sent missionaries to Iceland and was threatening the lives of Icelanders in Norway at the time, Thorgeir had to make a decision that rested on foreign politics. He also likely understood that "submission to Christ implied submission to [King Olaf.]"[55] The Icelanders' decision, according to Winroth, could "bypass King Olaf and his missionaries. That decision neutralized at least a part of the threat from the king; the Icelanders got their own church and accepted Christianity in a way that did not make them dependent on

Olaf."[56] This is very similar to the way Harald Bluetooth converted Denmark to a Christian kingdom, with a similar result that the conversion helped protect them from attacks and conquest in the name of religion. It also signified that they were not willing to submit to any outside authorities, although the Church hierarchy would soon find its way into Iceland.

The conversion story of Greenland is remarkably different than that of Iceland, but happened around the same time. In this situation the interpretation of the sagas cause some problems if not taken properly. The sagas refer to Erik the Red's son, Leif, sailing to Norway in 999 and staying in the court of King Olaf. The next year, 1000, Leif planned on returning to Norway, at which point Olaf requested that Leif convert the Greenlanders to Christianity, and Leif accepted the mission.[57] It is likely that Leif was baptized at King Olaf's court, and his crew likely followed his example. Leif then returned to Greenland, rescued a crew that had been shipwrecked, and "introduced Christianity to Greenland."[58] Or, if translated different, "[Leif] converted the country to Christianity."[59] While the meaning of the two translations is different, the end result is ultimately the same: Greenlanders began accepting Christianity and getting baptized, although they likely held onto a variety of pagan practices, as in Iceland. This would be typical as "religion was more fluid . . . with medieval people usually accepting one or a few things at a time, instead of an entire package of beliefs and practices when they 'converted.'"[60]

What is relayed in other saga evidence suggests that Greenland did accept Christianity quickly after Leif's return, with at least the exception of Leif's father Erik, but pagan practices certainly continued. *Erik the Red's Saga* continues to relay that Erik "was reluctant to give up his faith, but Thjodhild (Erik's wife) was quick to convert and had a church built a fair distance from the house. It was called Thjodhild's church and there she prayed, along with those other people who converted to Christianity, of whom there were many."[61] The sagas also confirm that some settlers to Greenland were Christian to begin with, including one man identified as from the Hebrides on Herjolf's ship who composed a verse to pray to God.[62]

Also in *Erik the Red's Saga* evidence exists that Thorkel, described earlier, hosted a "woman named Thorbjorg, a seeress . . . she was one of ten sisters, all of whom had the gift of prophecy."[63] It is unclear whether this event happened before or after Leif's voyage and return to Norway, as the sagas are not necessarily chronological. In order to perform her magic, Thorbjorg needed women who knew the *varðlokkur*—chants meant to draw spirits to the sorceress.

> Such women were not to be found. Then the people of the household were asked if there was anyone with such knowledge. Gudrid answered "I have neither magical powers nor the gift of prophecy, but in

> Iceland my foster mother, Halldis, taught me chants she called ward songs. . . . These are the sort of actions in which I intend to take no part, because I am a Christian woman . . . " Thorkel then urged Gudrid [to chant], who said she would do as he wished. The women formed a warding ring around the platform raised for sorcery, with Thorbjorg perched atop it. Gudrid spoke the chant so well and so beautifully that people there said they had never heard anyone recite in a fairer voice.[64]

Whether this scene took place before or after Leif's trip and subsequent conversion, a lot can be drawn from this episode. Gudrid, a Christian, still knew the pagan *varðlokkur* and was willing to perform them even though she was a Christian. Changing religion and its associated traditions did not happen immediately, and even blended pagan and Christian cultures together for a while. It also demonstrates the level of social acceptability to feast in a room with people of other religions and the ability of different religions to live together harmoniously in a small colony.

At this point a word of caution should be noted regarding the reliability of conversion stories in some sagas. All the sagas were written down well after Iceland was considered a Christian land. Ari, the excellent historian of *Landnámabók* and *Íslendingabók*, was a priest and included the genealogies that led to priests and bishops. The authors of *Erik the Red's Saga* and *The Saga of the Greenlanders* both conclude with genealogies that result in bishops as well. The main continental European source commonly referenced for describing the conversion process comes from Adam of Bremen, whose *History of the Archbishop of Hamburg-Bremen* has an extreme bias. One of Adam's goals in writing his *History* was to ensure that the archbishop in Bremen had control over the Scandinavian churches. Adam, therefore, claims his see is responsible for early missionary work in those countries, although no supporting evidence has yet been found. His information, much like that of Ari's, is drawn from other people who supposedly were present at different events. Adam and Ari both record that the first bishop of Iceland was Isleif, who was consecrated by the archbishop of Hamburg-Bremen in 1055.[65] Isleif's son, Teitr, was one of Ari's sources for his histories.

The description of Isleif being consecrated in Germany, supported by several sources, ties the Icelandic Church back to Hamburg-Bremen and Roman Catholicism. Norway also was part of the Roman Catholic Church. It can be assumed that Leif Erikson was baptized in Norway under King Olaf since many Vikings were willing to be baptized as needed to gain the favor of a king, as described earlier. The archaeological evidence suggests, however, there were people responsible for Christianity in Greenland that were not Roman Catholic, but rather were Celtic in origin. The difference between the Celtic and Roman are not based on beliefs, creed, or even practice, but instead on the social structure.

In Greenland's Eastern Settlement seventeen churches have been found and two, possibly three, in the Western Settlement.[66] It is suspected that a fourth church is waiting to be discovered in the Western settlement.[67] Recently, Keller identified that "seven churches of the Eastern settlement seem to have had a circular courtyard."[68] The Celtic Christians often constructed these types of churches with circular courtyards, while the Roman Catholic courtyard was typically rectangular.[69] Keller then suggests "that the circular churchyards are evidence of a Celtic Christian mission, being a forerunner for, or coterminous with, the mission from the Roman Catholic Church. . . . If so, the Church in Iceland and Greenland may have preserved certain features from a Celtic type of Christianity."[70] This also fits with the description that at least one settler, mentioned earlier, was a Christian from the Hebrides, likely with Celtic influences. So the archaeological evidence does not discredit the sagas, it simply emphasizes a different aspect of them.

The connection to Celtic Christianity compared to Roman Christianity revolves around the social structure. In Ireland, the origin of the Celtic Church, Christianity influenced the culture as much as the culture influenced Christianity. Rural Ireland was organized into tribes and clans when St. Patrick evangelized to the pagan civilization in the fifth century.[71] Because of the fall of Rome and the following disorganization, Church evangelization and mission work nearly ceased. After Patrick, Ireland saw no missionaries to follow up the conversion and transformation of society to fit the Roman Catholic norms. Instead a wave of monasticism swept across Europe and into Ireland's new religion.[72] The Celtic Church, as it came to be known, held the same beliefs as the Roman Catholic Church but was structured differently--monastic rather than diocesan.[73] As historian Addleshaw summarizes it, in the "bishop's office there was not that concentration of governmental functions as in the rest of Christendom . . . the bishops lived as members of a monastery; but it was with the abbots at the head of the monastery that the power lay."[74] The monastic nature and structure of Celtic Christianity was ideal for small communities attached via clans or kinship.

The Viking society that transferred to the Norse settlers in Iceland and Greenland was based on kinship and the role of *goðar*. The Celtic Church's model of monasticism was very similar model to the chieftaincy system, especially in Greenland which had fewer people and fewer communities than Iceland. The Roman Church had a hierarchy and social structure that was very similar to that of feudal Europe. The kingdoms of Europe were secular replications of this power structure, with the king on top. The early kings of Norway and Denmark tried to replicate this structure, and therefore were willing to adopt the Roman structure that accompanied Christianity. Iceland and Greenland were settled by people trying to escape this structure, which made the Celtic structure more adaptable to their particular situations.[75]

Either way, Christianity reached the islands of the North Atlantic and began to change the culture. It has been said, rather inaccurately, that the "Church was the great civilizer of the wild and blood-thirsty Norsemen."[76] While this is an exaggeration, the Norse settlers did adopt a variety of European activities necessary for the Church to function, particularly the book culture. Sorensen writes that "the most important tool of the church was the book. This was revolutionary, as it made it possible to preserve and transmit knowledge from remoter parts and times."[77] There is a distinct difference between a book culture and literate cultures, and the Norse were not certainly literate. The Norse were avid writers on runestones, but not on books.

The runes were used throughout Scandinavian culture on objects and memorial stones, including the Jelling stone found in Denmark. Historian and runic expert Gräslund notes that "in total, between five thousand and six thousand runic inscriptions are known today . . . mostly on runestones from the late Viking Age."[78] Common sense says it is also likely that most people could read the runic script. Because the runestones were "erected in such public places as along roads, at bridges, in cemeteries, and in other places where many people would see them, it seems likely that most people could read them, or there would have been little sense in putting them up."[79] Changing to the Latin script, therefore, should not have been too overly complicated or difficult. Indeed the change was necessary because Christianity is considered a literate religion, whose message, "as well as its theology and moral doctrine, was deeply rooted in the written word."[80] The evidence does suggest that the recent converts to Christianity did not abandon their runic script completely. Crosses from Herjoflsnes, in Greenland, contain Latin script as well as a hybrid runic script based on Latin letters.[81] The Norse runic language's continuation both for the vernacular as well as for the imported Latin language demonstrates the willingness to accept the new religion while holding on to traditional aspects of Norse culture.

The Church also changed the power structure over time in both Iceland and Greenland, but the change was very gradual. As late as the thirteenth century, Iceland and Greenland were "very decentralized and lacked any kind of political entities that could wield executive powers."[82] The power still rested with the *goðar* although the power that was available was being condensed into the hands of fewer families. There were more settlers located in the southern plains of Iceland, which meant more conflicts and a large exchange for power amongst *goðar*, as described earlier. The *goðar* needed money to maintain their position, and to solidify their power over longer periods of time they needed to find a reliable source of income. The solution to this problem was found in the Church.[83]

The Haukdælir family of southern Iceland seemed to be the first to successfully solve this problem. To summarize the events: Gizurr was baptized around 998, helped with the conversion in 1000, and soon sent his son to continental Europe for education. The son, Isleif, returned as a missionary priest and consequentially was asked to be Iceland's bishop. He then was consecrated by the Archbishop Adalbert of Hamburg-Bremen only fifty-five years after Iceland's conversion, and returned as Iceland's first bishop.[84] Isleif was from a wealthy family, his father and his mother's father were both *goðar*, and his father could afford to send him to the continent to be educated. All of this suggests that "the shaping of the Icelandic church was in the hands of the Icelandic aristocracy, and that the influence of foreign missionaries was slight."[85] In clever manipulation, the aristocracy gained a stronger financial foothold when they had built a church on their farm or donated part of their farm to the Church.

When a farm was donated to the Church, either a complete farm or a portion of the farm, the person donating the land could stipulate that their family and heirs were to manage the farmland for the Church. This ensured their family would continue to have a farmstead, especially the donations set up by *goðar*.[86] The Icelandic tithe system was divided into four parts. One part went to the bishop, one to the priest, one for the church property and maintenance, and one for the poor.[87] Those who donated property to a church or built a church on their property then collected the tithe portion for the church property and maintenance. Some could even claim two parts of the tithe, one for the land and one if the owner or a family member was a priest.[88] As Byock notes, "the increased wealth such families derived from control of church property hastened the evolution toward increased social complexity."[89]

Understandably, this structure and system of privatized churches was not favored by the Norwegian archbishop. Throughout the twelfth and thirteenth centuries, the Church tried getting churches out of private control. This is partly because Iceland's ecclesiastical structure did not match the ideal European model, but also because Church reformers needed to follow the papal lead and separate churches from secular control.[90] Taking churches away from private ownership asserted the pope's authority to appoint priests and bishops.[91] In 1297 the landowners were forced to sell their rather valuable property to church officials.[92] This had dire consequences for those whose families had given large quantities of land to churches. Large tracts of land were no longer readily available, and a constant source of income taken away.

The Greenland churches likely had the same type of set-up as their Icelandic counterparts, "it is thought to have been a decentralized system of privately owned churches."[93] Presumably this granted the landowner the same types of rights and tithe benefits as in Iceland. Also like Iceland, Norway ordered all private churches in Greenland be sold or eradicated. Similar to the situation in Iceland, "the Greenlandic farmer-magnates and church-owners, whose power was based on their control over those resources of society that were essential to the maintenance of cultural contacts with the outside world, had much at stake."[94] To enforce this, however, Greenland would need an ever constant bishop, which was never the case due to difficult travel and apathy on the part of the bishop. The first definitive time a bishop was in Greenland was the arrival of Bishop Helgi in 1210, and bishops were there intermittently until Bishop Alf died in 1378, at which point his replacement never sailed for Greenland.[95] This likely made enforcement of getting rid of private churches difficult, and there is no evidence one way or the other to show how fully the Greenlanders carried it out.

As the Church was taking away an important source of income for many *goðar*, the chieftaincy system started to fall apart in Iceland and was replaced by domains. Sigurðsson defines a domain as "an area with more or less fixed boundaries that involved authority over at least three chieftaincies and one spring assembly."[96] One of the earliest families to control a domain was the powerful Haukdælir family—the same family that included the first bishops of Iceland. This is not surprising since the Haukdælir family was likely able to collect a variety of tithes for a long period of time and soon acquired other chieftaincies and farms through marriage or purchase. This pattern holds true for other families as they controlled more land and seized more power.[97] Iceland ended up consolidating into eight domains.[98] As Iceland was controlled by fewer people, the families that controlled the domains found new ways to control the people in them and defend against other domains. Sigurðsson describes the change by analyzing the use of "trusted men, followers and the oath of allegiance that enabled them to manage the new, large units reasonably well. Trusted men acted as advisers and probably also as links in local government, while the followers were the bodyguards and police force."[99] This development likely stratified society more and made it easier for Norway's king to take over Iceland.

King Hákon Hákonarson (reign 1217–63) methodically planned to annex Iceland, even avoiding invasion because it did not fit his plan. The Norwegian Jarl Skúli had attempted an invasion of Iceland in 1220 as the result of a trade dispute, but was stopped by King Hákon's intervention. He instead planned to use Snorri Sturluson—then at the king's court—to convince the Icelanders that submission to Norway would be in their best interest. Historian Theodore Andersson describes the scene between Snorri and the king in 1220 when "King Hákon gave Snorri the title *lendr maðr* (district chieftain), that there was much discussion about Iceland."[100] Snorri then "got nowhere with his countrymen . . . he did not press the matter very hard."[101] King Hákon was then urged by Cardinal William of Savoy in 1247 to take Iceland, as it was "improper for Iceland to be the only country not to serve a king."[102]

The leaders of these large domains continued to contend with each other for land and prestige. By the time King Hákon took power in 1217, the Icelanders were on the verge of internal collapse. Norway's King

Hákon promised titles for different wealthy landowners in Iceland, sometimes referred to as a *stórgoðar* (large or great chieftain).[103] These *stórgoðar* continued to weaken one another. Eventually Gizur Thorvaldsson was given the title of *jarl* by King Hákon, and Gizur managed to win almost all of Iceland. Gizur also tried unsuccessfully to recreate in Iceland the feudal structure from the rest of Europe.

Iceland's northern and southern quarters finally submitted to King Hákon Hákonarson beginning in 1262 in an Althing decision known as *Gizurarsáttmáli*, with the rest of Iceland to follow within two years.[104] This name stems from the role Gizur played in setting up King Hákon's political conquest of Iceland. As with other titles given to Icelanders, "Gizur's jarldom proved to be only a temporary political experiment. It brought about no fundamental rearrangement of the social or political order, and its authority was never extended over the whole country."[105] The experiment did reaffirm the Icelander's dislike of the feudal structure. Between 1262 and 1264, King Hákon was able to offer Icelanders a reprieve from the chaos caused by the *stórgoðar*. He then destroyed the rest of the *stórgoðar* class and no more *jarls* were made.[106] The king died in 1263, after which his son King Magnus took over and continued mostly positive relations with Iceland.

Norway had promised to send six ships to Greenland and Iceland annually as part of their submissions, while Norway received taxes and tributary from both countries. Norway could also order people to travel to Norway for trials, against which the Icelanders unsuccessfully protested.[107] The advantages for Iceland were first and foremost the shipping guarantee—though not necessarily always fulfilled—as well as the protections that a kingdom offered. As Norway's economy fluctuated so did Iceland's, although Iceland actually saw an economic increase as the Norwegian influence waned in the fourteenth century. Iceland benefited because much of Norway's trade had to be rerouted around the Hanseatic sphere of influence, thereby forcing traffic to Iceland.[108]

Several disasters struck Scandinavia, which limited trading opportunities. The eruption of the volcano Hekla and earthquakes in the first half of the fourteenth century, coupled with rounds of the plague in Iceland greatly reduced resources and products used for trading. Economic historian Marcus notes that the Black Death in Norway had immediate implications for Norway's ability to trade, observing that "in 1347 twenty ships or more had wintered in Iceland. But in 1349 there was only one sailing to Iceland; in 1350, and again in 1355, no sailing at all."[109] Trade briefly resumed between Iceland and Norway near the turn of the fifteenth century, but again trade diminished. Marcus concludes that "only the providential arrival of merchantmen from England saved the Icelanders from a fate similar to that of the Norse colonists in Greenland."[110]

Although Iceland continued to maintain many of its own laws and customs, the Commonwealth period was over. Icelanders functioned mostly like they had before the *stórgoðar* had taken over and entered into conflict with each other.[111] Despite this semi-autonomous political situation formed between the Icelanders and Kings Hákon and Magnus, Iceland would continue to be subject to foreign powers until 1944.

Greenland submitted to Norway in 1261, although little exists describing how and why the Greenlanders decided to submit to Norway's king. What most scholars assume is the need to guarantee trade and contact in order to maintain the Greenland settlement, because Greenland was never completely self-sufficient.[112] The promise of six ships sailing to Greenland annually was necessary for Greenland's survival, as very few Greenlanders owned ships suitable for making the journey by the mid thirteenth century.[113] For some reasons discussed above in general and more discussed in Chapter Five, the ships did not always arrive in Greenland.

Overall, the power structures were very similar between Iceland and Greenland during this period of their civilizations. There was less power to be had in Greenland, but the power remained in the hands of a few farmers. The *goðar* were able to promote Christianity in both countries, and the transition from paganism to Christianity was remarkably smooth for both Iceland and Greenland. The conversion changed both the level of literacy and the structure of power. The private church system in both countries added to the wealth and prestige of the wealthy farmers and the *goðar* class, which was intentional and well planned by those who were successful. Little else is known of how Greenland's society changed, as there is little evidence for the later periods of its existence and not even the continual presence of church leaders. Iceland's political and social power continued to consolidate in the hands of *goðar* and *stórgoðar* until they continued to weaken each other, setting the stage for King Hákon to manipulate the remaining *stórgoðar* to his advantage. The Icelanders had little choice but to submit to Norway's king in order to stabilize their society and end the conflicts in Iceland.

NOTES

1. Christian Keller, "Vikings in the West Atlantic: A Model of Norse Greenlandic Medieval Society," in *The North Atlantic Frontier of Medieval Europe: Vikings and Celts*, ed. James Muldoon, vol. 3, The Expansion of Latin Europe, 1000–1500 (Surrey, England: Ashgate Publishing Limited, 2009), 28.
2. Haraldur Olafsson, "Sagas of Western Expansion," in *Vikings: The North Atlantic Saga*, ed. William W Fitzhugh and Elizabeth I Ward (Washington, D.C.: Smithsonian Institution Press, in association with the National Museum of Natural History, 2000), 145.
3. Patricia Pires Boulhosa, *Icelanders and the Kings of Norway: Mediaeval Sagas and Legal Texts* (Leiden: Brill Academic Pub, 2005), 193.
4. Keneva Kunz, trans., "The Saga of the People of Laxardal," in *The Sagas of Icelanders: A Selection* (New York: Penguin Books, 2001), 286.
5. Ibid., 413–414.
6. Ibid., 414.

7. Jesse L Byock, *Medieval Iceland: Society, Sagas, and Power* (Berkeley: University of California Press, 1988), 5.
8. Ibid., 4–5.
9. Jon Viðar Sigurðsson, *Chieftains and Power in the Icelandic Commonwealth* (Odense: University Press of Southern Denmark, 1999), 48.
10. William Ian Miller, *Bloodtaking and Peacemaking: Feud, Law, and Society in Saga Iceland* (Chicago: University Of Chicago Press, 1997), 29.
11. Kristen Hastrup, *Culture and History in Medieval Iceland: An Anthropological Analysis of Structure and Change* (Oxford ; New York: Oxford University Press, 1985), 120.
12. Sigurðsson, *Chieftains and Power in the Icelandic Commonwealth*, 207.
13. Ibid., 56.
14. Ibid., 84–85.
15. Ibid., 94.
16. Ibid.
17. Miller, *Bloodtaking and Peacemaking*, 29.
18. Else Roesdahl, *The Vikings* (New York: Penguin Books, 1998), 62.
19. Jesse L Byock, *Viking Age Iceland* (New York: Penguin Books, 2001), 174.
20. Roesdahl, *The Vikings*, 268.
21. Lars Jorgensen, "Political Organization and Social Life," in *Vikings: The North Atlantic Saga*, ed. William W Fitzhugh and Elizabeth I Ward (Washington, D.C.: Smithsonian Institution Press, in association with the National Museum of Natural History, 2000), 75.
22. Ibid.
23. Caroline Paulsen et al., *Archaeological Excavations at Qassiarsuk 2005-2006: Field Report (Data Structure Report)* (Bolungarvik, Iceland: North Atlantic Biocultural Organization, April 2007), 59.
24. Poul Norlund, *Viking Settlers in Greenland and Their Descendants during Five Hundred Years* (New York: Kraus Reprint Co., 1971), 24.
25. Ibid., 103.
26. Terry Gunnel, trans., "The Saga of Hrafnkel Frey's Godi," in *The Sagas of Icelanders: A Selection* (New York: Penguin Books, 2001), 450.
27. Hastrup, *Culture and History in Medieval Iceland*, 120.
28. Ivar Bárðarson, "A Fourteenth-Century Description of Greenland," trans. Derek Mathers, *Saga-Book* 33 (2009): 81.
29. Hastrup, *Culture and History in Medieval Iceland*, 122.
30. Keneva Kunz, trans., "Eirik the Red's Saga," in *The Sagas of Icelanders: A Selection* (New York: Penguin Books, 2001), 657.
31. Ibid., 658.
32. Gunnel, "The Saga of Hrafnkel Frey's Godi."
33. Miller, *Bloodtaking and Peacemaking*, 185.
34. Ibid., 181.
35. Thorstein's father insults Bjarni's offer at the end of the tale, but in doing so refers to "the promises of you chieftains." There is no other reference to Bjarni as a *goði*.
36. Anthony Maxwell, trans., "The Tale of Thorstein Staff-Struck," in *The Sagas of Icelanders: A Selection* (New York: Penguin Classics, 2001), 682.
37. Robert Cook, trans., *Njal's Saga* (New York: Penguin Classics, 2001).
38. Anders Winroth, *Conversion of Scandinavia: Vikings, Merchants, and Missionaries in the Remaking of Northern Europe* (New Haven, CT: Yale University Press, 2014), 24.
39. Ibid., 45.
40. Roesdahl, *The Vikings*, 158.
41. Jenny Jochens, "Late and Peaceful: Iceland's Conversion Through Arbitration in 1000," *Speculum* 74, no. 3 (July 1, 1999): 632, doi:10.2307/2886763.
42. Winroth, *Conversion of Scandinavia*, 143.

43. Preben Meulengracht Sorensen, "Religions Old and New," in *The Oxford Illustrated History of the Vikings*, ed. Peter Sawyer (Oxford: Oxford University Press, 2001), 220.
44. Winroth, *Conversion of Scandinavia*, 112.
45. Ibid., 114.
46. Widukind of Corvey, "Widukind of Corvey, The Deeds of the Saxons 3.65," trans. Anders Winroth, *Yale: Viking Sources in Translation*, 2006, https://classesv2.yale.edu/access/content/user/haw6/Vikings/Widukind.html.
47. Adam of Bremen, *History of the Archbishops of Hamburg-Bremen*, trans. Francis Joseph Tschan and Timothy Reuter (New York: Columbia University Press, 2002), 51.
48. Winroth, *Conversion of Scandinavia*, 113.
49. Niels Lund, "The Danish Empire and the End of the Viking Age," in *The Oxford Illustrated History of the Vikings*, ed. Peter Sawyer (Oxford: Oxford University Press, 2001), 165.
50. Ari Thorgilsson, "Íslendingabók," in *The Viking Age: A Reader*, ed. Angus A. Somerville and R. Andrew McDonald (Toronto: University of Toronto Press, 2010), 417.
51. Ibid., 418.
52. Ibid.
53. According to Ari, this happened in the year 1000. However, some scholars believe he may be off by a year and place the conversion at 999. Without any definitive evidence outside of Ari's history, the date of 1000 will be used here.
54. Thorgilsson, "Íslendingabók," 418.
55. Lund, "The Danish Empire and the End of the Viking Age," 164.
56. Winroth, *Conversion of Scandinavia*, 155.
57. Finn Gad, *History of Greenland: I. Earliest Times to 1700*, trans. Ernst Dupont, First Canadian edition (McGill-Queen's University Press, 1971), 41–42.
58. Angus A. Somerville and R. Andrew McDonald, eds., "The Saga of Eirik the Red," in *The Viking Age: A Reader* (Toronto: University of Toronto Press, 2010), 420.
59. Kunz, "Eirik the Red's Saga," 661.
60. Winroth, *Conversion of Scandinavia*, 133.
61. Kunz, "Eirik the Red's Saga," 661.
62. Keneva Kunz, trans., "The Saga of the Greenlanders," in *The Sagas of Icelanders: A Selection* (New York: Penguin Books, 2001), 636.
63. Ibid., 658.
64. Kunz, "Eirik the Red's Saga," 659.
65. Adam of Bremen, *History of the Archbishops of Hamburg-Bremen*, 218.
66. Jette Arneborg, "Greenland and Europe," in *Vikings: The North Atlantic Saga*, ed. William W Fitzhugh and Elizabeth I Ward (Washington, D.C.: Smithsonian Institution Press, in association with the National Museum of Natural History, 2000), 313.
67. Norlund, *Viking Settlers in Greenland and Their Descendants during Five Hundred Years*, 32.
68. Keller, "Vikings in the West Atlantic: A Model of Norse Greenlandic Medieval Society," 36.
69. Ibid., 36–37.
70. Ibid., 37.
71. Patrick V. Brannon, "Medieval Ireland: Music in Cathedral, Church and Cloister," *Early Music* 28, no. 2 (May 1, 2000): 193.
72. R. P. C. Hanson, "The Reaction of the Church to the Collapse of the Western Roman Empire in the Fifth Century," *Vigiliae Christianae* 26, no. 4 (December 1, 1972): 282, doi:10.2307/1583559.
73. Brannon, "Medieval Ireland," 193.
74. G.W.O. Addleshaw, *The Pastoral Structure of the Celtic Church in Northern Britain* (York, England: St. Anthony's Press, 1973), 1.
75. Keller, "Vikings in the West Atlantic: A Model of Norse Greenlandic Medieval Society," 36–37.

76. Carl H. Meinberg, "The Norse Church in Medieval America," *The Catholic Historical Review* 11, no. 2 (July 1, 1925): 186.
77. Sorensen, "Religions Old and New," 222.
78. Anne-Sofie Gräslund, "Religion, Art, and Runes," in *Vikings: The North Atlantic Saga*, ed. William W Fitzhugh and Elizabeth I Ward (Washington, D.C.: Smithsonian Institution Press, in association with the National Museum of Natural History, 2000), 67.
79. Ibid., 67–68.
80. Sorensen, "Religions Old and New," 222.
81. Lisbeth M. Imer, "The Runic Inscriptions from Vatnahverfi and the Evidence of Communication," *Journal of the North Atlantic* 2, no. sp2 (January 1, 2009): 75, doi:10.3721/037.002.s209.
82. Orri Vésteinsson, *The Christianization of Iceland: Priests, Power, and Social Change 1000-1300* (Oxford: Oxford University Press, 2000), 12.
83. Ibid., 15–16.
84. Ibid., 20; Adam of Bremen, *History of the Archbishops of Hamburg-Bremen*, 218.
85. Vésteinsson, *The Christianization of Iceland*, 24.
86. Sigurðsson, *Chieftains and Power in the Icelandic Commonwealth*, 108.
87. Byock, *Medieval Iceland*, 92.
88. Ibid.
89. Ibid., 94.
90. Birgit Sawyer and Peter Sawyer, *Medieval Scandinavia: From Conversion to Reformation, circa 800-1500* (Minneapolis: University of Minnesota Press, 1993), 118–119.
91. Ibid., 112.
92. Arneborg, "Greenland and Europe," 315.
93. Jette Arneborg, "Norse Greenland: Reflections on Settlement and Depopulation," in *Contact, Continuity, and Collapse: The Norse Colonization of the North Atlantic*, ed. James H Barrett (Turnhout, Belgium: Brepols, 2003), 172.
94. Arneborg, "Greenland and Europe," 315.
95. Ibid., 311.
96. Sigurðsson, *Chieftains and Power in the Icelandic Commonwealth*, 64.
97. Helgi Thorlaksson, "The Icelandic Commonwealth Period: Building a New Society," in *Vikings: The North Atlantic Saga*, ed. William W Fitzhugh and Elizabeth I Ward (Washington, D.C.: Smithsonian Institution Press, in association with the National Museum of Natural History, 2000), 185.
98. Sigurðsson, *Chieftains and Power in the Icelandic Commonwealth*, 67.
99. Ibid., 82–83.
100. Theodore M. Andersson, "The King of Iceland," *Speculum* 74, no. 4 (October 1, 1999): 927, doi:10.2307/2886968.
101. Ibid., 928.
102. Ibid.
103. Byock, *Viking Age Iceland*, 3–4.
104. Boulhosa, *Icelanders and the Kings of Norway*, 87.
105. Byock, *Viking Age Iceland*, 351.
106. Ibid.
107. G. J. Marcus, "The Norse Traffic with Iceland," *The Economic History Review*, New Series, 9, no. 3 (January 1, 1957): 416, doi:10.2307/2591132.
108. Ibid., 417.
109. Ibid., 418.
110. Ibid., 419.
111. Byock, *Viking Age Iceland*, 351–353.
112. G. J. Marcus, "The Greenland Trade-Route," *The Economic History Review*, New Series, 7, no. 1 (January 1, 1954): 71, doi:10.2307/2591227.
113. Guðmundur J. Guðmundsson, "Greenland and the Wider World," *Journal of the North Atlantic* 2, no. sp2 (January 1, 2009): 70, doi:10.3721/037.002.s208.

FOUR

Trade and Travel

It is no secret that the Viking Age witnessed Scandinavians traveling throughout much of the known world. They traveled from Scandinavian homelands through continental Europe and the Mediterranean, down eastern Europe's and western Asia's river systems, and throughout the British Isles. What originated with raiding ended in trading and exploration. This extensive network built by the Viking warriors and traders benefited the residents of Iceland and Greenland, as they were able to join the trade networks with goods new and unique to the existing markets. The practice of setting out on Viking voyages to distant lands in order to raid and plunder also set the stage for how the Norse settlers in Greenland dealt with unknown people they encountered, both in Greenland and North America.

The Viking heritage of the settlers was important in several aspects. One impact was the shift from being raiders to being traders. The Vikings for the most part controlled this trade network. "Eventually the Viking tactic of raiding and trading resulted in a vast trade network that they controlled—and that greatly expanded the areas of Viking influence."[1] The Viking trade networks started in Scandinavia, where major ports like Hedeby, Birka, Kaupang, and later Trondheim operated as places where merchants could peaceably trade and exchange goods.[2] The trade networks soon moved across the Baltic, continental Europe, and into the Mediterranean, connecting Scandinavia with other Europeans and Arab traders.[3] The Greenlanders and especially the Icelanders made vast use of this trade network.

Trade with Europe was essential to the livelihood of Icelanders, and vital for the Greenland's survival. One condition set in place by the Icelanders during their submission to Norway during 1262/64 was that Norway must send six ships every year.[4] This clause could be a guarantee to maintain trade connections with Norway. It also could, as has been suggested, have been put in place due to a shortage of ships capable of carrying cargo between Iceland and other countries.[5] Whether Iceland suffered from a lack of ships or not, the clause is evidence that Iceland needed to be connected to Norway in order to trade.

If Iceland needed to guarantee trade with Norway in order to maintain connections, Greenland needed to guarantee trade in order to help maintain existence. Keller suggests that Greenland "could not base its survival on the supplies of the comparatively few ships that negotiated the North Atlantic, particularly in regard to edibles."[6] He does concede, however, that "we can conclude that the ships provided the Greenlanders with strategic resources for their survival, and luxury articles for their aristocracy."[7] It was possible for the Greenlanders to survive without trade and contact with Europe, as will be discussed in chapter five, however it was nearly impossible to maintain much of their way of life without the occasional support offered by trade. In a culture based on gift giving as a key to honor and power, as described earlier, a lack of new supplies via trade could damage that system.

Many of the items imported into Greenland and Iceland can be classified as typical, everyday goods that fulfill basic needs, though not necessarily for subsistence. "Iron and other materials as well as timber and tar for houses and boats were important, and after the conversion to Christianity, the newly established church needed various goods like wax, linen, and wine."[8] In the *Saga of the People of Laxardal* the discussion between Thorkel and Norway's King Olaf—described in length in chapter 3—references Thorkel's need for timber from Norway. Iceland and Greenland both were in constant need of wood, the few natural sources of which were destroyed because of the vast amounts of land used for farming.[9] "The transformation of natural woodland to landscapes heavily eroded by overgrazing is documented in the sedimentary, floral, and faunal record."[10] Much of the wood available on the islands was driftwood, suitable for small scale projects but not for large construction projects like churches or ships. At the recently excavated "Farm Beneath the Sand" site in Greenland, Berglund discovered more wood than he expected to find and notes that "some of the wood was riddled with holes made by shipworms and could be identified as driftwood but other wood was undamaged and may have come from Vinland or Norway."[11] Both the written and archaeological evidence points to the common nature of wood and timbers being imported to Iceland and Greenland.

Trade is not the only way goods made their way to Iceland and Greenland. The sagas record a number of people who arrive from various different countries bringing luxury items—no doubt recorded to bring glory and honor to the traveler if they settled and the families they visited. Bolli Bollason, a figure found in the *Saga of the People of Laxardal*, "brought with him a great deal of wealth from abroad and may treasures given him by princes ... he wore only clothes of scarlet or silk brocade and all his weapons were decorated with gold ... he wore a suit of silk brocade given to him by the emperor of Byzantium."[12] The *Saga of Gunnlaug Serpent-Tongue* also traces how a poet, the title character Gunnlaug, collects wealth throughout Scandinavia and the British Isles. Gunnlaug composed and recited poems about various rulers, gaining gifts each time he pleased a ruler. The short conversation held between King Sigtrygg Silk-beard of Dublin (reigned 996–1042) and his treasurer gives insight to the rewards Gunnlaug later received:

> The king thanks Gunnlaug for the poem, and summoned his treasurer. "How should I reward the poem?" he asked. "How would you like to, my lord?" the treasurer said. "What kind of reward would it be if I gave him a pair of knorrs?" the king asked. "That is too much, my lord," [the treasurer] replied. "Other kings give fine treasures — good swords or splendid gold bracelets — as rewards for poems." The king gave Gunnlaug his own new suit of scarlet clothes, an embroidered tunic, a cloak lined with exquisite furs and a gold bracelet which weighed a mark.[13]

The saga also relays that Gunnlaug received axes and other riches from earls to kings, including King Ethelred of England.[14]

Beyond the physical items that moved from continental Europe and the rest of the world into Iceland and Greenland, new cultural ideas traversed the North Atlantic along with traders. The Latin script moved into both Iceland and Greenland with the adoption of Christianity, even operating alongside runic script, as has already been described. Loan words from other languages, especially Celtic languages, made their way into Norse place names. Fashion also changed in Iceland and Greenland to stay current with continental European fashions. Berglund describes the influence of European fashion on Iceland and Greenland by writing that "it is clear that the textiles were expertly made in accordance with the European taste of the day."[15] The best evidence of this is from the graveyard excavated in Herjolfsnes in 1921.[16]

In 1921 the Commission for Scientific Research in Greenland and the National Museum of Copenhagen sponsored a dig, led by Norlund, to excavate a graveyard by the Herjolfsnes church remains. Norlund and his group discovered well preserved items underneath a layer of frozen ground, enough "objects in the course of the following five weeks that they filled twelve large cases."[17] Most important among these discoveries were the ordinary, everyday clothes found as opposed to special or ecclesiastical clothing. A total of seventeen liripipe hoods were found, which "better than anything else ... marks the men of the fourteenth century."[18] The liripipe hood is identified by its long, ribbon-like tail that extends from the top of the back of the hood, and was extremely popular across fourteenth century Europe.[19] Also in the graves were a number of caps, usually worn under the hoods. In particular one cap is considered evidence of some contact near the sixteenth century—about a thirty centimeter tall Burgundy cap. This cap was the style worn by Europeans during the reign of France's Louis XI (reign 1461-83).[20] The clothing styles represent some form of communication and exchange of ideas between Greenland and other Europeans, although no record of contact exists after the first decade of the fifteenth century.

Goods also traveled from Greenland and Iceland to the rest of Europe, many by way of Norway and Denmark. The historian Guðmundur J. Guðmundsson divides these goods into two parts: bulk and exotic.[21] The bulk goods included "sheep, goat, and cow hides . . . together with sealskin, walrus skin and walrus ivory."[22] The Greenlanders especially made use of walrus skin as a useful and very desirable trade item. They made a type of heavy rope by "cutting the skin up into long shreds round and round the animal; the long shreds were then twisted into ropes that were so strong that they could be used as anchoring and mooring cables. As a consequence, walrus skin was a much-coveted article."[23] While not mentioned specifically in any primary sources, it appears that *vaðmál*, a type of Greenlandic homespun wool, was also sold extensively in Europe.[24]

The exotic items sold by Greenlanders to the rest of European merchants included walrus tusks, narwhal horns, and polar bears—both living and dead. Another popular commodity was the Icelandic falcon for hunting and the Greenlandic white falcon.[25] The walrus tusk was extremely valuable in Europe as the import of elephant ivory was declining in the Middle Ages.[26] This was beneficial to the Greenlanders because the first half of the Greenland settlement enjoyed a warmer climate. If this is so, then the walrus was likely often present near the Norse settlements and therefore relatively easy to acquire.[27] The narwhal tusk also was a high-priced trade item because many Europeans believed it to be a unicorn horn—something the Greenland merchants probably did not correct. Polar bears, especially alive but even their skin, were prized gifts among European monarchs and nobility.[28] The records indicate that many of these exotic goods were sent to the churchmen in Europe as Greenland's payment of tithes.[29]

Again, the primary sources provide a wealth of information on the different items sold or given by Icelanders and Greenlanders and the type of value they had on the continent. The most detailed description of this relationship appears in the *Tale of Audun from the West Fjords*. Audun sailed from Iceland to Greenland and gave everything he had for a live polar bear. His goal was to travel to Norway and then to Denmark, ultimately giving the gift to Denmark's king. Upon Audun's arrival in Norway, "King Harald was soon told that a bear, a great treasure owned by an Icelandic man, had arrived there. The king immediately sent men to summon him."[30] Audun refuses offers from King Harald for the bear, including the king's offer to pay double whatever price Audun had paid.

When Audun makes it to Denmark he gives the polar bear to King Svein as a gift, and the king in turn gives him "a great deal of silver."[31] Later in the story Audun returns to the king as a humble beggar, after which the king has him nursed back to health. When Audun leaves, the king gives him more gifts, including a ship, which the saga notes is "repayment for the bear."[32] He also receives more money and a gold arm band.

While not exactly a trading expedition, Audun's tale illustrates the value placed on such an exotic animal. It also demonstrates how the value of the animal increases as Audun takes it farther south. It was no doubt unusual for somebody to bring a polar bear to Norway, but King Harald does not find it as exotic as King Svein does in Denmark. To King Svein, the live polar bear is worth silver plus a ship capable of traveling to Iceland, likely a knorr. The gift is also memorable, as shown when a sickly Audun is remembered by Svein as the man who gave him a polar bear.

Beyond trading, the residents of Iceland and Greenland appeared to travel extensively. Trips to Norway seem almost commonplace, at least among the wealthy, but evidence suggests that the non-wealthy also traveled. After the introduction of Christianity, a variety of people are mentioned as making pilgrimages to Rome, Constantinople, and a handful even to Jerusalem. Some Icelanders and Greenlanders joined Viking raids while others joined military groups heading to a crusade. A small number of Greenlanders even sailed west and landed in North America nearly five centuries before Columbus.

While both Iceland and Greenland lay a considerable distance from continental Europe, records indicate many Icelanders and Greenlanders did travel throughout Europe and into Asia. Audun, the traveler with a polar bear in Denmark, made an overland pilgrimage to Rome.[33] Flosi, one of the men who helped burn Njal's family in his house near the end of *Njal's Saga*, also took a pilgrimage to Rome as part of his penance and settlement for his part in the series of murders. Flosi also took a landroute to Rome, while another main character from the end of the saga, Kari, made a pilgrimage to Rome and then "returned by the western route and took over his ship in Normandy."[34] Men are not the only characters to travel to Rome or other holy cities. Aud and Gunnhild of *Gisli Sursson's Saga* "went to Hedeby in Denmark, took the Christian faith and then went on a pilgrimage to Rome. They never returned."[35]

By the brief descriptions given, the saga authors made the assumption that his audience knew the best routes to Rome and the different return routes. This implies the routes are described in other sagas and stories that are non-extant, or enough people had traveled those routes so that the audience as a whole had a general idea of the paths taken. The passages about pilgrimage to Rome also demonstrate that, whether the characters truly took these great religious journeys or if they were tactics the saga authors used to build up reputations and display religious prominence and standing, the act of pilgrimage was possible and regular. Audun is described as traveling "with a group of pilgrims."[36] It was neither an independent nor a rare journey, but one common to the saga audience because it must have happened regularly.

Norsemen traveled beyond Rome, including to Constantinople. Eyvind, the last character to die in *The Saga of Hrafnkel Frey's Godi* is described at the very beginning as a merchant who "went abroad to Norway . . . from there he went to other countries, and stopped in Constantinople where he gained great honour from the King of Greeks. He stayed there a while."[37] Eyvind the merchant traveled in order to gain wealth since his profession was selling things. The Mediterranean, specifically Constantinople, was an ideal market for exotic Icelandic goods. Thorkel, another character in the same saga, is quoted as saying "I'd been abroad for six years, and been to Constantinople. I am a sworn follower of the Greek Emperor."[38] Thorkel is probably making a reference to being a Varnagian, a Norse mercenary hired by the Byzantine rulers.

The *Tale of Halldor Snorrason II* also describes an Icelander who served in Byzantium. The saga opens by saying that "Halldor Snorrason had been in Constantinople with Harald, and had come west with him, from Russia to Norway."[39] Halldor travelled as a mercenary with Harald Hardrada, and later appears in charge of a ship and leads warriors. He was probably a member of the Varangians that served the Byzantine emperor, as it is relayed in *Harald Sigurdarson's Saga*. The saga explains that Harald "arrived in [Constantinople], he went to see the queen and entered her service as a mercenary soldier . . . before long the Varangians allied themselves with Harald, and formed up with him and his men whenever there was a battle. Eventually, Harald became leader of all the Varangians."[40] While serving the emperor and his queen, Harald and the Varangians traveled throughout the Mediterranean, including visiting Jerusalem. Halldor of the *Tale of Halldor Snorrason II* is likely the same Icelandic Halldor thrown into prison with Harald before they were rescued by a local woman the next night.[41] Harald and his men are described as some of the richest men ever seen in the North Atlantic as a result of their conquests around the Mediterranean.

Those in Iceland and Greenland did not simply travel back and forth with Norway and continental Europe. In a bit of coincidence or parallelism, both Greenland and Iceland were discovered by sailors being blown off course. The discovery of Vinland, located in North America, was also by accident. Two sagas describe the discovery: *Saga of the Greenlanders* and *Erik the Red's Saga*. They differ slightly in the process of events regarding the discovery, but they both describe the land and the Skraelings similarly. In *Saga of the Greenlanders*, Bjarni Herjolfsson sees Vinland and tells people about it when he eventually arrives in Greenland. Leif Erikson then sails to and explores the land Bjarni spotted.[42] *Erik the Red's Saga* features Leif being blown off course on his return from Norway, and discovers it has a very inviting climate and set of resources.[43] In both cases, Leif is the first European to actually set foot on North American soil.

The discovery of Vinland by Norse voyagers matters a great deal to the course of history, as opposed to some who argue that knowledge of Vinland did not exist outside of the Norse, and "consequently had little or no influence on the new phase of Atlantic exploration which began during the fifteenth century."[44] The reality of the issue is that the area of Vinland was known through parts of Europe, as the eleventh century German author Adam of Bremen references voyages there. Some may argue that Christopher Columbus knew of the Norse voyages to Vinland before he took his voyage, although that story seems doubtful, especially since he never appears to have used that information when appealing for funding to sail westward.[45] What is far more important, however, is the impact the contact between North America and Greenland had for both the natives in North America and the farmers in Greenland. This contact creates trade partners that provide much needed material in Greenland and lays the foundation for interactions between other Native Americans and Europeans.

The first contact between Native Americans and the Norse appears in the *Saga of the Greenlanders*, after one of Erik's son's, Thorvald, sails to and explores Vinland.

> Thorvald and his companions went ashore. He then spoke: "This is an attractive spot, and here I would like to build my farm." As they headed back to the ship they saw three hillocks on the beach inland from the cape. Upon coming closer they saw they were three hide-covered boats, with three men under each of them. They divided their forces and managed to capture all of them except one, who escaped with his boat. They killed the other eight and went back to the cape. On surveying the area they saw a number of hillocks further up the fjord, and assumed them to be settlements.[46]

The first contact results in conflict, with eight of nine present natives being killed. This scene is followed by a short dream sequence that ends in a warning to Thorvald that danger was looming. More hide-covered boats approached and a brief battle ensued, resulting in Thorvald's death from an arrow.[47]

This scene gives a variety of information regarding the Vinland voyages. The Greenlanders had hoped to set up farms, as Thorvald picked an ideal farmstead, apparently thinking they must have been alone for quite a while. The brief description of the natives encountered by Thorvald gives clues to which groups the Norse clashed with. Kolodny suggests the "nine men encountered on the beach were an Algonquian hunting party."[48] Jones also points to the description as identifying an Algonquian boat compared to an Eskimo kayak.[49] More importantly it offers a view into the perception of the pre-Christian Norse.

The same saga informs the reader shortly after that scene that "in those days Christianity was still in its infancy in Greenland."[50] Norse mythology included a variety of different creatures who could appear in human or near-human form, with dwarves or trolls being common. "One way to distinguish the human from the nonhuman was by the use of an iron weapon: A spirit or supernatural being could not be killed by an iron blade, while a human could."[51] Since the people under the boats looked similar to other humans, but not exactly like anybody they had met before, skepticism and fear of the supernatural may have led to the bloody conflict.

The next encounter between Norse and native ends much more positively, but also offers extremely interesting information about their interactions. Thorfinn Karlsefni, a Norwegian who married Leif's sister-in-law, Gudrid, led a voyage to Vinland.

> After the first winter passed and summer came, they became aware of natives. A large group of men came out of the woods close to where the cattle were pastured. The bull began bellowing and snorting very loudly. This frightened the natives, who ran off with their burdens, which included fur pelts and sables and all kinds of skins. They headed for Karlsefni's farm and tried to get into the house, but Karlsefni had the door defended. Neither group understood the language of the other ... [Karlsefni] sought a solution by having the women bring out milk and milk products. Once they saw these products the natives wished to purchase them and nothing else.[52]

The natives knew what kind of goods the Norse would value—skins and furs. This implies that the natives had been watching the Norse since they first arrived, although the Norse appeared unaware they were watched.[53] The communication barrier also proved to be an issue as the Norse did not understand the significance of trading weapons as a peace offering. Instead, the Norse refused the weapons trade and sent out milk instead. The meeting ended positively though and set up another exchange of goods between the two groups. [54]

Karlsefni's time in Vinland ends after a violent third encounter.[55] He is left with little option but to depart for Greenland after realizing "they were unwilling to woo and unable to conquer."[56] He soon returns to Greenland "taking with them plenty of the land's products—grapevines, berries, and skins."[57] Leif and Thorvald's men took grapevines and berries as well when they returned to Greenland, in part for recognition that they had traveled to Vinland and in part for the honor the exotic goods could bring. The goods available in North America to the Norse become the main reason they continue to travel there, as setting up permanent settlements seems unreasonable after the attempts by Leif, Thorvald, and Karlsefni.

North America supplemented vital resources for much of Norse Greenland's existence, resources which usually shipped from Norway. Although known foremost for grapes, North America offered the Norse vast amounts of much needed timber. As has been described by a number of archaeologists and historians, Greenland basically had access to a small amount of short birch trees. They relied heavily for construction and shipbuilding on "driftwood and on lumber imported from Norway. The timber that they could obtain from North America provided therefore an important supplement to their limited supply of wood."[58] Lumber was so important it was listed as being brought back to Greenland in one of two expeditions in *Erik the Red's Saga* and in three of four expeditions in *Saga of the Greenlanders*. *Erik the Red's Saga* goes as far as identifying at least one tree as a maple, although Leif brings a variety of types home.[59] The last written record of a connection between North America and Greenland is found in the Icelandic Annals. According to the Annals, a storm had blown a ship off course that had been returning to Greenland from Markland, likely for lumber supplies.[60] The archaeological evidence also points to Greenlanders utilizing American lumber. Chests have been discovered on Greenland made of "larch or tamarack, a tree that grows abundantly in Labrador and Newfoundland but does not exist in Scandinavia."[61]

The physical evidence for interaction is sparse, but as the archaeological work continues the evidence will slowly grow. In the area bordering Markland, the name given to a forested region of North America by the Norse, there have been two finds "of small objects made from smelted copper, products of a technology unknown to aboriginal peoples of Northern America."[62] Discoveries have been made of copper fragments around the east coast of Hudson Bay and the Hudson Strait (c. 12–13th century), a bronze balance piece on Ellesmere Island (c. 13–14th centuries), and iron fragments from the west coast of Hudson Bay (c. 12–14th centuries).[63] Though regular trading patterns probably never developed, the archaeological evidence suggests that contact and trade continued throughout the fourteenth century.[64]

Two discoveries still remain a mystery: a Norse penny found in Maine and a Native American arrowhead found in Greenland. The arrow point was found near a cemetery at Sandnes, in Greenland's Western Settlement. This is the only piece of Native American work found in Greenland, but it comes from a type of stone found only in North America and not in Greenland. It could have been an object of trade, a gift of a weapon—as gifting a weapon had symbolic importance for the Native Americans—or it could have come from a battle or even a battle wound.[65] The penny is of even more uncertainty than the arrowhead.

The penny was discovered in 1956 by amateur archaeologists but ignored by them and others until the mid-1970s, when a 1978 article was published about the coin. The coin was first identified as British in origin, but the English coin expert subsequently identified it as Norwegian.[66] While one side's Short Cross motif was common among Norwegian coinage, the reverse image of an animal matches no other coins. However, a neutron analysis matched the low silver content to coins struck in Norway during the reign of Olav Kyrre, who reigned from 1066 to 1093.[67] The penny also appeared to have a hold punctured in it, likely being worn as a pendant or necklace.[68]

How the penny made it from Norway to Maine will likely never be known. The main possibilities include a Norwegian ship traveling down the Canadian coast and joining the extensive Native American trade network near Naskeag Point, where the coin was found, or being traded much earlier and moving down the coast in the hands of Native Americans. The first theory, backed by McKusick and Wahlgren,[69] supports the belief that the Norse explored and traded into New England. The second theory, maintained by Cox,[70] constrains the Norse contact to the region north of the St. Lawrence River. Regardless of which theory may be true, the penny's mysterious and uncertain arrival in Maine confirms the Norse had contact with people in North America—people who remembered them.

The Norse wrote down their version of contact within a couple generations of the events, but the Native American versions were not written down until the 1800s when a Baptist missionary, Silas Tertius Rand (1810–99), collected stories from the Mi'kmaq, an Algonquian tribe located near Nova Scotia and Prince Edward Island.[71] One of the stories he recorded tells of the first Europeans encountered by the Mi'kmaq, called "The Coming of the White Man Revealed" or "The Dream of the White Robe and the Floating Island." The story begins "when there were no people in this country but Indians, and before any others were known, a young woman had a singular dream."[72] None of the elders could interpret her dream until a floating island arrived with bears that turned into men and a man dressed in white. Kolodny describes in detail how this relates to the Norse arrival in North America and the symbolism involved. The first sentence of the story points out that only Native Americans were known in North America, nobody else. The island with trees is a ship with masts, the bears represent danger or even battles, and the man dressed in white fits the Mi'kmaq "medicine wheel," connecting the color white with the direction where the sun rises.[73] This story could serve as a warning to be careful of visitors from the east or a remembrance of early conflict and uncertain relations with the Norse, as found in the sagas.

However, in case one wants to take the descriptions word-for-word, Kolodny offers an alternative interpretation. The Norse commonly wore long capes of animal skin topped with a hood and turned fur side in, sometimes even wearing a bear-tooth necklace or pendant—suggesting their description as bears to be well founded. The caution is that "Norse seafarers and the later Basque fishermen and French explorers appeared to dress pretty much alike. They all wore heavy linen or wool shirts and pants, leather jerkins (or leather aprons in the case of the Basque), wool capes, or capes with various animal skin linings, and most were bearded."[74] The version ultimately told to Rand in the late 1800s was likely a combination of eight centuries of contact between Native Americans and Europeans. The Mi'kmaq and Norse stories of contact appear to complement each other and the archaeological evidence.

The role this contact between North America and Scandinavians had, as well as the general outcomes of the Norse in the North Atlantic, has been the subject of some debate. As the medieval historian J.R.S. Phillips incorrectly suggests, "there was little or no knowledge in late medieval Europe of the lands which we now know as North America."[75] This sentiment is echoed by Muldoon, who writes "in the long run, the Viking advance into the Atlantic had little significance."[76] Enterline, on the other hand, suggests that this knowledge of North America had permeated continental Europe and was the groundwork for the Age of Exploration.[77] Fitzhugh and Ward also credit the Viking Age explorers as having "redefined the shape of Europe."[78] The contact and trade networks established by the Norse were vital to expanding the worldview of Europe and necessary to the survival of Iceland and, for a time, Greenland.

The concept that Norse trade and contact with the outside world is unimportant takes away from the Norse accomplishments and the spread of ideas around Europe. Phillips suggests that the insignificance comes from an incorrect geographical view of the world. Medieval Europeans, including Scandinavians, believed the known land was encompassed by one large ocean and Greenland was north of Norway. Not far away from Greenland were the islands of Markland, Helluland, and Vinland, and Vinland actually was near Africa.[79] The incorrect geographic view argument in and of itself is faulty because that argument could extend to all geographic knowledge being meaningless and useless until modern satellite mapping technology was used. If nothing else the knowledge that there are more lands or islands, some of which are inhabitable, inspired "practical men to act."[80] As G.J. Marcus highlights, these discoveries and contacts by the Norse created the first transoceanic voyage that continued for several centuries.[81]

Muldoon argues that from his perspective the new lands, even including Iceland, had little to offer and Vinland "held out no great promise."[82] Both the new lands and the trade routes from the North Atlantic to the rest of Europe were vital for all of Scandinavia, which was witnessing rapid population growth. These new lands—Iceland, Greenland, and Vinland—helped prevent overcrowding.[83] More importantly, the Markland timber resources allowed necessary lumber materials to flow to Greenland, reducing the burden placed on Norway. The North Atlantic trade also opened up new markets—a new opportunity for Europeans to sell goods in Iceland and Greenland and new exotic goods to be sold in Europe.[84]

NOTES

1. Christopher D. Morris, "The Viking Age in Europe," in *Vikings: The North Atlantic Saga*, ed. William W Fitzhugh and Elizabeth I Ward (Washington, D.C.: Smithsonian Institution Press, in association with the National Museum of Natural History, 2000), 100.
2. Else Roesdahl, *The Vikings* (New York: Penguin Books, 1998), 120–126.
3. Lotte Hedeager, "From Warrior to Trade Economy," in *Vikings: The North Atlantic Saga*, ed. William W Fitzhugh and Elizabeth I Ward (Washington, D.C.: Smithsonian Institution Press, in association with the National Museum of Natural History, 2000), 84–85.
4. Patricia Pires Boulhosa, *Icelanders and the Kings of Norway: Mediaeval Sagas and Legal Texts* (Leiden: Brill Academic Pub, 2005), 129.
5. See Boulhosa, 128-130, as well as Bruce E. Gelsinger, *Icelandic Enterprise: Commerce and Economy in the Middle Ages* (Columbia, SC: University of South Carolina Press, 1981).
6. Christian Keller, "Vikings in the West Atlantic: A Model of Norse Greenlandic Medieval Society," in *The North Atlantic Frontier of Medieval Europe: Vikings and Celts*, ed. James Muldoon, vol. 3, The Expansion of Latin Europe, 1000-1500 (Surrey, England: Ashgate Publishing Limited, 2009), 40.
7. Ibid.
8. Guðmundur J. Guðmundsson, "Greenland and the Wider World," *Journal of the North Atlantic* 2, no. sp2 (January 1, 2009): 67, doi:10.3721/037.002.s208.
9. Sveinbjorn Rafnsson, "The Atlantic Islands," in *The Oxford Illustrated History of the Vikings*, ed. Peter Sawyer (Oxford: Oxford University Press, 2001), 120.
10. Paul C Buckland, "The North Atlantic Environment," in *Vikings: The North Atlantic Saga*, ed. William W Fitzhugh and Elizabeth I Ward (Washington, D.C.: Smithsonian Institution Press, in association with the National Museum of Natural History, 2000), 153.
11. Joel Berglund, "The Farm Beneath the Sand," in *Vikings: The North Atlantic Saga*, ed. William W Fitzhugh and Elizabeth I Ward (Washington, D.C.: Smithsonian Institution Press, in association with the National Museum of Natural History, 2000), 297.
12. Keneva Kunz, trans., "The Saga of the People of Laxardal," in *The Sagas of Icelanders: A Selection* (New York: Penguin Books, 2001), 419.
13. Katrina C. Attwood, "The Saga of Gunnlaug Serpent-Tongue," in *The Sagas of Icelanders: A Selection* (New York: Penguin Books, 2001), 575.
14. Ibid., 580.
15. Berglund, "The Farm Beneath the Sand," 300.
16. Ibid.
17. Poul Norlund, *Viking Settlers in Greenland and Their Descendants during Five Hundred Years* (New York: Kraus Reprint Co., 1971), 107.
18. Ibid., 118–119.
19. Ibid., 118–122.
20. Ibid., 124–125.
21. Guðmundsson, "Greenland and the Wider World," 67.
22. Finn Gad, *History of Greenland: I. Earliest Times to 1700*, trans. Ernst Dupont, First Canadian edition (McGill-Queen's University Press, 1971), 85.
23. Ibid.

24. Guðmundsson, "Greenland and the Wider World," 67.
25. Ibid., 68.
26. Ibid.
27. Gad, *History of Greenland*, 85.
28. Ibid., 57.
29. Keller, "Vikings in the West Atlantic: A Model of Norse Greenlandic Medieval Society," 40.
30. Anthony Maxwell, trans., "The Tale of Audun from the West Fjords," in *The Sagas of Icelanders: A Selection* (New York: Penguin Classics, 2000), 717.
31. Ibid., 719.
32. Ibid., 721.
33. Ibid., 719–720.
34. Robert Cook, trans., *Njal's Saga* (New York: Penguin Classics, 2001), 309.
35. Martin S. Regal, "Gisli Sursson's Saga," in *The Sagas of Icelanders: A Selection* (New York: Penguin Books, 2001), 557.
36. Maxwell, "The Tale of Audun from the West Fjords," 719.
37. Terry Gunnel, trans., "The Saga of Hrafnkel Frey's Godi," in *The Sagas of Icelanders: A Selection* (New York: Penguin Books, 2001), 439.
38. Ibid., 447.
39. Terry Gunnel, trans., "The Tale of Halldor Snorrason II," in *The Sagas of Icelanders: A Selection* (New York: Penguin Classics, 2001), 685.
40. Snorri Sturluson, "Harald Sigurdarson's Saga," in *The Viking Age: A Reader*, ed. and trans. Angus A. Somerville and R. Andrew McDonald (Toronto: University of Toronto Press, 2010), 321.
41. Ibid., 323–324.
42. Keneva Kunz, trans., "The Saga of the Greenlanders," in *The Sagas of Icelanders: A Selection* (New York: Penguin Books, 2001), 636–640.
43. Keneva Kunz, trans., "Eirik the Red's Saga," in *The Sagas of Icelanders: A Selection* (New York: Penguin Books, 2001), 661.
44. J. R. S. Phillips, *The Medieval Expansion of Europe* (New York: Oxford University Press, 1988), 164.
45. James Robert Enterline, *Erikson, Eskimos, and Columbus: Medieval European Knowledge of America* (Baltimore: Johns Hopkins University Press, 2004), 205.
46. Kunz, "The Saga of the Greenlanders," 642.
47. Ibid., 643.
48. Annette Kolodny, *In Search of First Contact: The Vikings of Vinland, the Peoples of the Dawnland, and the Anglo-American Anxiety of Discovery* (Durham, NC: Duke University Press Books, 2012), 58.
49. Gwyn Jones, *The Norse Atlantic Saga: Being the Norse Voyages of Discovery and Settlement to Iceland, Greenland, and North America*, 2nd edition (New York: Oxford University Press, 1986), 133.
50. Kunz, "The Saga of the Greenlanders," 644.
51. Kolodny, *In Search of First Contact*, 59.
52. Kunz, "The Saga of the Greenlanders," 646–647.
53. Kolodny, *In Search of First Contact*, 64.
54. Kolodny, *In Search of First Contact*, 65.
55. The third encounter proves to be tragically ironic, as it is the result of a Norseman thinking a Native had tried taking an axe. During the encounter the natives get a Norse axe and do not view it as a weapon of war. It is pointed out they likely only saw it as useful for cutting down trees or were curious about the metal.
56. Jones, *The Norse Atlantic Saga*, 135.
57. Kunz, "The Saga of the Greenlanders," 648.
58. Oddvar K. Hoidal, "Norsemen and the North American Forests," *Journal of Forest History* 24, no. 4 (October 1980): 202.
59. Kunz, "Eirik the Red's Saga," 661.
60. Jones, *The Norse Atlantic Saga*, 136.

61. Hoidal, "Norsemen and the North American Forests," 203.

62. Patricia D. Sutherland, "The Norse and the Native Americans," in *Vikings: The North Atlantic Saga*, ed. William W Fitzhugh and Elizabeth I Ward (Washington, D.C.: Smithsonian Institution Press, in association with the National Museum of Natural History, 2000), 240.

63. Ibid., 247.

64. Ibid.

65. Ibid., 239.

66. Steven L. Cox, "A Norse Penny from Maine," in *Vikings: The North Atlantic Saga*, ed. William W Fitzhugh and Elizabeth I Ward (Washington, D.C.: Smithsonian Institution Press, in association with the National Museum of Natural History, 2000), 206.

67. Marshall McKusick and Erik Wahlgren, "The Norse Penny Mystery," *Archaeology of Eastern North America* 8 (Fall 1980): 3.

68. Cox, "A Norse Penny from Maine," 207; McKusick and Wahlgren, "The Norse Penny Mystery," 4.

69. McKusick and Wahlgren, "The Norse Penny Mystery," 4–5.

70. Cox, "A Norse Penny from Maine," 207.

71. Kolodny, *In Search of First Contact*, 281.

72. Ibid., 283.

73. Ibid., 285–287.

74. Ibid., 292.

75. Phillips, *The Medieval Expansion of Europe*, 182.

76. James Muldoon, "Introduction," in *The North Atlantic Frontier of Medieval Europe: Vikings and Celts*, ed. James Muldoon (Farnham, England: Ashgate, 2009), xvii.

77. Enterline, *Erikson, Eskimos, and Columbus*, 194–195.

78. William W Fitzhugh and Elizabeth I Ward, "Celebrating the Viking Past: A Viking Millenium in America," in *Vikings: The North Atlantic Saga*, ed. William W Fitzhugh and Elizabeth I Ward (Washington, D.C.: Smithsonian Institution Press, in association with the National Museum of Natural History, 2000), 352.

79. Phillips, *The Medieval Expansion of Europe*, 183.

80. Enterline, *Erikson, Eskimos, and Columbus*, 195.

81. G. J. Marcus, "The Greenland Trade-Route," *The Economic History Review*, New Series, 7, no. 1 (January 1, 1954): 71, doi:10.2307/2591227.

82. Muldoon, "Introduction," xvii.

83. Hoidal, "Norsemen and the North American Forests," 200.

84. Rafnsson, "The Atlantic Islands," 132.

FIVE
Troubled Times and Decline

In 1261 the Greenlanders submitted to Norwegian authority, and that included banning trade with all other countries. Norway had guaranteed regular trading and shipping traffic to Greenland, but few ships successfully made the voyage. After Norway and Denmark united in 1380, Denmark was in charge of the trade with Greenland and trade and shipping traffic dwindled even more.[1] Even the bishops assigned to Greenland attempted to avoid traveling there. Greenland lacked enough wood to construct ships worthy enough to make it to Norway.[2] The only written evidence of Greenland after their submission comes from the priest Ivar Bárðarson, who was writing mid-fourteenth century, and a letter from two other priests relating to a wedding they witnessed in 1408. That wedding party, part of a ship blown off course between Norway and Iceland, left in 1410 with other Icelanders to go back home. That was the last time any European saw a Norse Greenlander alive.[3]

Iceland also encountered problems after submitting to Norwegian authority in 1262/64, but managed to survive. Subsistence issues impacted Iceland during the Little Ice Age, as evidenced by the decline in the number of particular insects found in and around middens.[4] As a territory of Norway and later Norway-Denmark, Iceland's economy began to suffer, spending the next four centuries as a "relatively impoverished rural province in the kingdom of Norway–Denmark with a population fluctuating around 50,000."[5] Iceland adapted to the changing situation and economy by joining the fish supply chain that provided food for urban continental markets.[6] Icelanders also relied on fish to help counter the soil erosion happening due to overgrazing and land mismanagement.[7] Iceland suffered through two rounds of Black Death in the fifteenth century as well.[8] Late Medieval Iceland managed to survive through a variety of problems, some similar to the problems encountered by Greenland. Iceland proved to be resilient to the various events encountered, though not necessarily growing. The fourteenth century created pivotal moments when the survival of both countries hung in the balance.

Norway's role as a key trade partner between Iceland, Greenland, and the rest of Europe clearly declined in the fourteenth century. This decline happened when the Hanseatic League, which was mostly made up of German merchants, took charge of the foreign trade system that Norway had controlled. Norway was left to manage only its own regional trade network.[9] Iceland and Greenland no longer had the opportunity to sell goods through Norway to larger markets, but instead their market size dwindled to only the Scandinavian countries. Those countries, in return, needed much less from the Norse colonies. This also corresponds to the time when walrus ivory was losing its appeal in Europe. After the Crusades had ended, elephant ivory flowed more freely into Europe again, especially because elephant ivory was larger and purer than the ivory offered by walrus tusks. The surplus of walrus tusks that flooded the European market at this time contributed to the drop in prices and profit.[10] Shortly after this combination of events pushed the desire for walrus tusk down, Greenland's Western Settlement disappeared, taking with it important hunting ground and the possibility of collecting more walrus tusk to attract merchants.[11]

Iceland's troubles weren't only economic strife as a result of declining trade, but environmental factors also ravished the island near the beginning of the fourteenth century. After surviving nearly ten years of plagues and famine, Iceland's geologic activity spiked. Hekla, Iceland's most active volcano, erupted in 1300. Making Hekla even more destructive is its nature as a glaciovolcano, or a volcano covered in ice.[12] Glaciovolcanoes can build up steam before the eruption actually happens, leading to more violent eruptions.[13] Jones points out that "between 1306 and 1314 only two years were free of volcanic action, earthquake, or plague, with their resultant loss of life and destruction of the means of existence."[14] The glaciovolcano Oræfajokul erupted in 1362 with an explosion compared to that of Mount Vesuvius.[15] Scientists believe the dangerous increase in geologic activity resulted from changing climactic conditions, and this period corresponds with a shift from the Medieval Warm Period to the Little Ice Age.[16]

These different events compounded Iceland's problems in the early fourteenth century. The eruptions and earthquakes damaged or destroyed farms and wiped out herds. During the eruptions the toxic gases killed both people and animals, with birds falling dead out of the sky.[17] The gas and ash fanned out and covered much of Iceland, with ash and acid from the 1300 Hekla and 1362 Oræfajokul eruptions reaching at least Sweden.[18] The resultant ash fell on pastures and destroyed what grazing lands were still available. Those pastures not ruined by volcanoes were being destroyed by erosion.

Tephra analysis in Iceland reveals the increased rate at which soil erosion occurred after the settlement period. This increase was due to the variety of livestock brought to Iceland by settlers. The livestock "could strip dwarf trees of leaves and bark . . . tore up roots . . . [and] could rapidly roll back forests and prevent regeneration."[19] The soil erosion hampered agricultural and grazing practices in Iceland, and led to decreased production and sustainability. One way the Icelanders managed soil erosion was through the practice of landscape resilience, or a reduction of livestock grazing and population in exchange for alternate sources of protein—marine life such as sealing in this instance. Iceland's adaptations lasted only decades at a time, but impacted the environment for centuries, allowing them to survive while Greenland failed.[20]

The decline of grazing and farming capabilities due to soil erosion contributed to the growth of Iceland's cod trade. Cod live in the cold waters of the North Atlantic, although the largest are found in offshore waters, and large spawning cod can be found off Iceland's coast. An advantage of the cod compared to other fish is the lack of oil in its flesh. As environmental historian Hoffmann explains, "the oil-free flesh of fish caught on simple baited lines, beheaded, split, and gutted, dries without salt in the open, chill Arctic air to make stockfish."[21] The stockfish appears little known to most medieval Europeans, although it appeared regularly in the late fourteenth century cookbooks.[22] This corresponds to the increasing devastation that took place on Icelandic farms and their need to find alternative methods of survival coupled with the loss of natural fish habitats and overfishing across continental Europe.[23] The Icelanders began commercializing their offshore cod fisheries and exporting it to continental markets before the English and later the Hanseatic merchants took over the trade.[24] The Icelandic shift towards cod as a means of survival is another example of a socioeconomic adaptation that balanced out the decreasing production of the Icelandic farms.

The Greenlanders could not adapt to changes and problems the same way Iceland could, although a number of different theories have emerged over the last century for why Greenland's settlement failed. Unfortunately, very little evidence exists to piece together what happened or even when something happened to the Norse Greenlanders. The theories from leading researchers range from a mass migration to complete destruction by outside attackers to climate change. Recently some of the main schools of thought are working together to reconstruct the closing decades of Greenland's existence using a more all-encompassing approach.

Ivar Bárðarson was a Norwegian priest who was sent to Greenland around 1341 and stayed there approximately twenty years as a type of fill-in bishop and manager of church lands. His description of Greenland is considered to be mostly accurate, and is important because he described the scene in the Western Settlement after it was abandoned. Bárðarson stated that the Western Settlement is "completely unpopulated, and in front of [the settlement] stands a large church which is called Stensnes Church; this was for a time the cathedral and bishop's seat. Now the natives have all of the [Western Settlement]. There are many horses, goats, cows and sheep, all wild, and no people, Christian or heathen."[25] In the next paragraph, Bárðarson describes why he was at that place. He "was one of those selected by the Lawman to go to [the Western Settlement] among the natives and drive them out."[26]

Norlund relays the story of Jon Greenlander, an Icelander who around 1540 found a "dead man lying face downwards on the ground. On his head was a hood, well made, and otherwise clothes both of frieze cloth and of sealskin. Near him was a sheath-knife, bent and much worn and eaten away."[27] No other record of any European seeing a Greenlander—dead or alive—exists. Future explorations failed to materialize or looked in the wrong places, although they likely were all dead before Jon Greenlander arrived.

There is an Inuit story that describes a conflict between the Norse Greenlanders and the Inuit, although it is not meant as an explanation for the demise of the settlement. The story, "Ungortok the Chief of Kakortok," relays a conflict between a Norse chieftain and an Inuit. Ultimately the chieftain, Ungortok, is killed by the Inuit Kaisape in a scene very similar to the feud system. At one point in the story the Inuit trapped a number of Norse in a house and proceeded to burn the house down and all the residents therein.[28] For a while this story was used as evidence for an Inuit invasion and attack on the Norse settlers, although it was since reconsidered and can be considered akin to sagas and tales about feuds.

Another Inuit story offers a different, yet catastrophic, version of events. According to a legend passed down for generations, the Norse settlers in Greenland were the victims of pirate attacks. The attacks began with three ships of English or German origin, which evolved into an entire fleet the following year. The pirates wrought havoc and destruction on the Norse village, causing the residents to flee. The Inuit fled the next time the pirates arrived, taking with them many women and children. The story ends with the escaped Inuit and Norse returning to find "that everything had been carried away, and houses and farms were burned down so that nothing was left."[29] The archaeological evidence, however, shows only a single building destroyed by fire or extreme violence, thereby countering the Inuit story of destruction via pirates.[30]

Early theories go back to Icelandic bishop Gisli Oddsson, who in the early seventeenth century claimed that the Greenlanders decided to leave and moved to North America, marrying into Native American tribes.[31] Oddsson's theory still plays into different concepts, although even early professional historians began to discredit the intermarriage theory. In 1906 Stefansson concludes that the "Icelandic colony in Greenland was destroyed by the Eskimo rather than assimilated with them. Apparently there are few, if any, traces of early Scandinavian influence upon the culture of the natives."[32] Most modern historians, described below, discredit both theories as the cause of Norse Greenland's extinction.

An early leading theory on the topic came from Norlund in the 1930s. Norlund uses skeletal remains to support the idea that the population "was doomed to extinction, first and foremost owing to malnutrition . . . we must also take it that the race was degenerate owing to intermarrying . . . they had become an inactive flock of debilitated individuals, undersized and deformed."[33] Norlund cited as evidence two women's graves, one a middle-aged hunchback and the other a shorter woman with scoliosis and a rachitic disease.[34]

Norlund also describes the Greenland settlement as hazardously close to the edge of extinction, with any long-lasting or sudden event having the ability to derail it. Norlund does offer climate change as a possibility for the extinction of Greenland, but has little evidence to base a sound theory on. Instead, a major piece of his theory—along with his evidence of the residents' declining health and physical statures—is the destruction of vegetation due to a lasting plague of caterpillars. The caterpillars (*Agrotis oculta*) were responsible for destroying the food source of the livestock, which in turn devastated the livestock population and the dairy-producing population. This abrupt decline in the traditional farming patterns proved too much for the Greenlanders, and coupled with the already declining physical stature of the inhabitants reduced the ability of the Norse to reproduce.[35] Norlund concludes from that series of events "the race was doomed."[36]

Describing the Greenland population as "doomed" effectually blames fate and destiny for their ultimate destruction, no matter the course of events that caused the eventual end of Norse Greenland. For Norlund, the extreme focus on animal husbandry and the necessary crops to sustain that lifestyle kept the Norse from quickly adapting to different changes, such as the caterpillar plague that ravaged their food supply. But their dependence on that system also kept them from slowly changing their diets, resulting in stunted growth and various diseases. The fate of Norse Greenland, according to Norlund, had already been sealed and was waiting for some change to finish off its destruction.

Approximately 460 medieval Norse remains have been found in Greenland to date. Recent analyses of the skeletal remains no longer fit Norlund's theory of massive malnutrition and widespread disease. The two remains he described as depleted, diseased, and "doomed" are the only two remains that demonstrate malnutrition and damaging diseases, the rest of the remains being consistent with other medieval remains throughout Europe.[37] Regarding Norlund's caterpillar concept, pollen analysis confirms the presence of swarms of caterpillars, but it also shows the domesticated animals brought by the Norse to Greenland were just as destructive. Indeed, a regular pattern of grass and crop destruction followed by soil erosion appears in Greenland and Iceland, with the soil erosion being a modern concern as well.[38] A plague of caterpillars, while important, only helped to expedite the erosion pattern already happening in Greenland.

In 1966 Helge Ingstad, the historian and explorer who helped discover the L'Anse aux Meadows settlement, postulates that the Greenland Norse quickly moved to other countries. The Western Settlement moved to North America due to the caterpillar plague and the encroaching Inuit.[39] Ingstad explains the Western Settlement had "been living under a certain pressure. They were few and scattered, and would not have been able to put up so firm a resistance as [the Eastern Settlement]. If in addition to this their living-conditions were deteriorating, they may well have been tempted to try their luck in some other country."[40] He also cites Bárðarson's account as supporting evidence for the explanation of voyaging to other lands. As mentioned earlier, Bárðarson witnessed "many horses, goats, cows and sheep, all wild."[41] Ingstad interprets this as the result of small ships that could carry little extra cargo, forcing the Greenlanders to leave behind whatever they could not take with. They then crossed the Davis Strait and headed towards the areas of Markland and Vinland, around modern day Baffin Island and Labrador.[42]

This migration period from the Western Settlement to North America took place around the mid fourteenth century, according to Ingstad. This dating fits with the description and timeline of Bárðarson's excursion to the Western Settlement. Ingstad also cites the curious Icelandic Annals entry in 1347, mentioned earlier in Chapter Four, that a ship had been blown off course between Markland and Greenland and ended up in Iceland. The general theory is that the ship was getting lumber for Greenland.[43] Because the time frame seems to fit with the Western Settlement's migration, Ingstad suggests that the ship was not getting lumber from Markland but rather the ship carried Greenlanders bound for Markland.[44] The Greenlanders' survival in North America probably was unlikely, but Ingstad points out that "from the account of the Vinland voyages we remember that it was a perilous thing for a small community to land on Indian shores."[45]

While the primary source evidence could be interpreted to fit his ideas, the available archaeological evidence does not support Ingstad's theory that Norse residents left Greenland, bound for North America. The small evidence of contact between Norse and Native Americans is substantial enough to indicate contact did take place, as discussed in the previous chapter. There is not enough evidence to demonstrate a permanent settlement from Greenland to North America. The L'Anse aux Meadows site can be ruled out as the location the Greenlanders settled in the fourteenth century, as the radiocarbon, artifacts, and building styles date to the turn of the eleventh century.[46] No other Norse settlements have been found in North America, nor have any Norse graves or bones been found. It also is interesting that nobody from the Western Settlement stayed behind or traveled to the Eastern Settlement and reported the emigration of the entire settlement—something Bárðarson as the bishop's representative would certainly have recorded.

Ingstad's theory that the depopulation of the Eastern Settlement resulted from pirate attacks is more plausible. English pirate raids are known to have attacked and plundered Iceland and Greenland in the fifteenth century, even leading to a peace treaty between the king of Denmark-Norway and England.[47] Ingstad pieces together various evidence to prove his point of pirate invasions, attacks, and the burning of major buildings to the ground. First he cites a papal letter of 1448 describing pirate attacks in Greenland thirty years earlier—thereby dating the attacks to 1418.[48] Other evidence used by Ingstad is the remains of the Gardar cathedral and the immense amounts of charcoal, indicating destruction by fire.[49] Another piece of evidence that Ingstad uses for the destruction of Greenland's Eastern Settlement by pirates is the Inuit story about English pirate attacks on the Greenlanders.

The concept that the Norse were compelled to leave for other lands is plausible. The arrival of hostile ships around Greenland in the thirteenth and fourteenth centuries is also probable because pirate ships are known to have attacked Iceland. However, the destruction of the Eastern Settlement by pirates is too extreme, as modern archaeologists attribute nearly none of the destroyed buildings to attacks or fire, and certainly not to massive fires.[50] This theory fails to show up in the literature written after the 1970s, when new enthusiasm in archaeology revisited sites and began collecting new evidence.[51]

Many theories have since developed that put the main cause for Greenland's demise as climate change. Specifically the reference is to the Little Ice Age. The Little Ice Age is the name given to the centuries-long temperature drop that happened throughout the Northern Hemisphere and followed the Medieval Warm Period. The Medieval Warm Period lasted from the ninth century into the thirteenth century, which coincides with the Norse expansion into the North Atlantic and settlement of both Iceland and Greenland. During this time, researchers note "the North Atlantic may have been a calmer, warmer, and somewhat more stable environment than it was to become after ca. 1300."[52] It is also thought this period offered an average temperature increase of one degree Celsius above normal.[53] The Medieval Warm Period ended with an uptick in volcanic activity that increased the ice formation on seas and in glaciers, beginning the Little Ice Age.[54]

Scientists date the beginning of the Little Ice Age to the late thirteenth century, resulting in an average temperature drop of one degree Celsius below average for the next six centuries.[55] Because the Little Ice Age followed the Medieval Warm Period, the average temperature fell two degrees. The average degree difference is enough to drastically shorten the amount of time available to grow grazing grass, and eliminates any serious attempt at cereal production.[56] The specific concept of the Little Ice Age was not available to Norlund, whose work and publications came before the Little Ice Age was first proposed by the geographer and glaciation expert Matthes in 1939.[57] Since that time, the Little Ice Age and climate change in general appears as an almost constant factor for the demise of Norse Greenland in the theories of many historians and archaeologists. Different scholars have put the emphasis and impact of the changing climate on different aspects of the Greenland society.

One result of the Little Ice Age is the supposed blocking off of shipping lanes. Early in the debate on Greenland, G.J. Marcus wrote that shipping was relatively unaffected. In 1954 he writes "in spite of the increasingly severe ice conditions, communication between Norway and Greenland was kept up intermittently down to the early years of the fifteenth century.... At irregular intervals a *knörr* would brave the perils of the long transatlantic voyage."[58] According to Marcus the trade declines because of the strict foreign trade ban imposed on both Iceland and Greenland by the Norwegian king. The Greenlanders were wary of trading with anybody else because they did not want to "send off the goods belonging to the Crown which had for long been accumulating in the storehouses."[59] The trade then took a bigger hit due to the Black Death in Norway in the mid fourteenth century. He also argues that the archaeological evidence—clothing found in graves at Herjolfsnes—demonstrates trade must have happened into the fifteenth and possibly up to the sixteenth centuries.[60]

Greenland historian Finn Gad, publishing his *History of Greenland* in 1971, provides one of the first interdisciplinary approaches to explaining the demise of Norse Greenland, although influence by Norlund and Ingstad is evident in his work. Gad suggests that Bárðarson's account of the Western Settlement accurately reflects a climate of conflict between the Norse residents and the Inuit slowly moving down the coast of Greenland.[61] Most remarkable to Gad is that Bárðarson's party arrived shortly after the depopulation of the Western Settlement, noting that "untethered cattle and sheep could not be expected to survive the bitter cold of the winter."[62] Using an entry in the Icelandic Annals from 1379 that claims two Inuit attacked the Greenlanders and killed eighteen people, Gad concludes "from the middle of the century onwards the Norsemen and the Eskimos must have regarded each other as enemies."[63] Gad also uses the conflict between the Norse and the Inuit as an explanation for blocking off the Norse access to the *Norðrestur*, or the northern hunting grounds rich in walrus and narwhal that was vital to the Greenland trade. The inability to reach the *Norðrestur* was "disastrous for the entire Norse population in Greenland."[64]

In Gad's estimation, climate change is not the cause of Greenland's demise, but it caused the depopulation and set the stage for the final moments of the Norse in Greenland. The deteriorating weather conditions shortened the growing season but aided soil erosion. He describes the scene at a Vatnahverfi farm where skeletal remains were found in a room in the house, not buried but instead almost in a hallway. The resident tried surviving on whatever animals still lived on the farm, unable to grow crops and feed the animals. The farmer continually got weaker and sicker until taken by death in the middle of his house. This is the concept that Gad believes played out throughout farms and communities in Norse Greenland.[65]

The last surviving Norse in Greenland was likely around Herjolfsnes, the best port in Greenland. Citing Norlund, Gad uses the two deformed skeletons found at Herjolfsnes as indicative of the declining population's health.[66] Ingstad's views are echoed as well, with part of the cause for Greenland's demise coming at the hands of pirates and marauders.[67] Gad then weaves an interesting story that some of the few surviving Greenlanders were scared off in the fifteenth century by pirates and they tried sailing towards other lands they deemed safer but died at sea. Their death at sea is fairly logical, considering the lack of resources for building seaworthy ships and by the fifteenth century the "Norse Greenland farmer was not an expert navigator."[68] Women and children ran off with the Inuit, and the remaining residents were "killed by the Basques and thrown into the sea, which was the easiest way to dispose of a murder victim."[69]

While Gad worked on a more modern, multifaceted, interdisciplinary approach and included climate change as a cause leading to the downward spiral of Greenland's residents, his theories are rather distant to today's scholars. The population is known to be much healthier than Gad describes, and the evidence for a mass murder and burning in any part of Greenland does not exist. No Norse traits have been found in any Inuit remains, making the theory the Norse women and children lived with and intermarried the Inuit nearly impossible.[70] The conflicts and war-like climate described by Gad based on the comment that eighteen men were killed by Inuit can also be explained by the lack of commentary on other Norse-Inuit interactions. Gulløv, an anthropologist, suggests that the conflicts likely arose from one party trying to steal or dishonor the other party. This conclusion is drawn from the number of goods and items that were traded between the two groups, no records of which were ever written. What would have stood out, and therefore be recorded, would have been a conflict that ended in violence.[71]

However, Gad's assertion that the loss of *Norðrestur* is important to changing trade conditions still matches some current thought on the issue. This event is a precursor to the need of the Norse to shift towards marine life as a means of subsistence, which is mostly unsuccessful in

Greenland. Gad's depressing description of a lonely farmer with nobody to bury him is also fairly reasonable. McGovern highlights farms in the Western Settlement that show people living off of last-resort types of foods, including the "scrawny winter hare and grouse as last-ditch famine food."[72] A hunting dog was found "with cut marks on some of its bones,"[73] indicating it likely turned into a meal for a starving farmer. McGovern also shows that carrion-eating flies were present throughout houses in the last stages of those farms, and not mostly contained to cooking and eating areas.[74] It could be hypothesized that the death of both animals and humans occurred throughout the houses and the bodies must have remained for an extended period of time, at least long enough for the flies to arrive.

Noted North Atlantic researcher and archaeologist Jette Arneborg places the cause of Greenland's failure as the result of climate change and non-sustainable farming practices, but places the blame on the people themselves.[75] Their responsibility was to adapt, but she notes that "Norse adaptations to the changing Greenlandic climate ultimately failed . . . the failure to adopt Thule culture hunting practices has been noted as especially crucial."[76] Arneborg views the concept that the Norse failed to adapt from a trade perspective, not just a subsistence perspective like other scholars have done. The explanation she offers, therefore, is much more economical than agricultural.

Arneborg explains that the Norse survived due to their ability to provide exotic goods to Europe—such as walrus tusk—and the goods from Europe were necessary to sustain their farming practices—including iron tools such as sickles.[77] This system of hunting and trade also was the power base for their social structure and even their chieftaincy system. A failing trade system due to poor climate for shipping, a decrease in the number of ships, and goods no longer desired in Europe coupled with the loss of northern hunting grounds meant disaster for Greenland's society.[78] Therefore the changing climate impacted the ability to receive and trade goods, although their goods were no longer desired by Europeans. As she notes though, what was available were large marine animals that could have been better exploited as a food resource.

Similar to Arneborg, archaeologist Joel Berglund places the emphasis for decline and eventual failure of Greenland on the economic situation in Greenland and cessation of trade. The basis for the economic change was a change in climate, noting "it is conceivable that the settlements were ravaged by a succession of 'bad years' (unstable climate and insufficient fodder) which resulted in some emigration in the fringe areas and in a reduction of livestock in the central areas."[79] Berglund describes the Greenland economy as livestock based and dependent on supplying trade goods desired by Europe—such as polar bears and walrus skin and ivory. This was subsidized by a reliance on fishing and hunting sea mammals.

An interesting aspect of his theory is the impact of overgrazing and erosion as a leading factor in the decline of the Norse settlements in Greenland. Assuming the Western Settlement did begin to fail and slowly migrated into the Eastern Settlement, the population in the Eastern Settlement would have grown. Berglund follows this line of reasoning and states that "the Eastern Settlement people became too numerous to live on the available resources . . . the subtle balance between resting, growing, and grazing periods had been disturbed."[80] The climate changes forced people to leave the Western Settlement, complicating and compromising the balance between the Eastern Settlement and its resources. Once the balance was changed, the Greenlanders could not get it back.

One of the biggest challenges to this theory comes from the seemingly simple letter regarding the 1408 wedding. That letter made no mention of overpopulation in the Eastern Settlement and expressed no concern about a decreasing food supply. Berglund suggests this is because the migration and population change was gradual, and the area the wedding took place in was near Greenland's largest and wealthiest port. Therefore, the Icelandic visitors to the area would not necessarily notice the change.[81]

Writing his first essay in 1986, Berglund doubted and dismissed Bárðarson's account of the Western Settlement's desertion in the mid-fourteenth century. Bárðarson's account was flawed and contradictory to other evidence.[82] However, once the Farm Beneath the Sand was discovered and archaeological work started—led by Berglund—more of Bárðarson's account became more accurate. Bárðarson, for example, describes the scene of roaming livestock in the Western Settlement as "many horses, goats, cows and sheep, all wild, and no people."[83] Berglund changed his mind on at least part of Bárðarson's account when he writes:

> The quantities of animal manure that lay in all rooms in this abandoned farm appear to confirm the story of untethered domestic animals. They would have been unable to take all their animals with them, and those that were left behind would have stayed near the farm for shelter until it disappeared . . . one of the last creatures to live on the farm—a goat, its skeleton with skin and hair preserved more or less intact in the permafrost—was found under a collapsed wall.[84]

The geological dating though places the farm's last inhabitants near the end of the fifteenth century, nearly a century later than Bárðarson's account. The evidence at the farm also shows no signs of distress or panicked flight from the home. Items must have been packed and taken in an orderly fashion when the family decided life on the farm was no longer sustainable.[85] While the mystery of the Farm Beneath the Sand is intriguing, and offers a wonderful glimpse into different aspects of life on a

Greenland farm, it does not give many clues to the demise of the Norse in the Western Settlement. It does, however, add evidence to Berglund's earlier assertion that the climate caused economic and subsistence changes that eventually could not be accounted for.

Archaeologist and historian Christian Keller suggests that the loss of *Norðrestur* and its economic impact was the major cause that led to Greenland's downfall, accompanied by a disconnect with the Roman Catholic Church. Beyond the understandable loss of food supplies and local economic impact, without *Norðrestur* there was no reason for foreign merchants to visit regularly, if at all. Keller combines this with the absence of a bishop in Greenland since 1378. Keller describes those consequences as "the line of consecration was broken, and the religious foundation of the society must have eroded. In a society experiencing isolation, climatic deterioration and eventually, lack of strategic resources, the loss of religious comfort and solace was no less than a disaster."[86]

Another multifaceted approach to the extinction of the Norse Greenlanders is advanced in one of the anthropologist and bioarchaeologist Thomas McGovern's early essays. In 1980, McGovern describes the Little Ice Age as a survivable time for the Norse, but their actions in the face of climate change led to their demise. He explains that the Norse were extremely dependent on their cattle surviving winter and beginning to graze in early spring and on the meat supplies that came from *Norðrestur*. He also views Greenland's society as extremely stratified, with the elite and church leaders having tremendous impact on the interactions of Norse and Inuit. These factors led to the Norse choosing not to adapt but rather intensifying their already existing strategies of survival.[87]

The differences between the earlier theories of Arneborg, Keller, and McGovern are rather minute. Arneborg suggests the climate impacted the hunting and trading opportunities, destroying the power base of society and a major food source. Keller argues that the loss of hunting grounds due to climate change helped sever communication with merchants and the Church, resulting in a crumbling society unable to adapt. McGovern explains the Norse failure in terms of adaptation to the changing resources due to the climate deterioration and the inability or unwillingness of the social elites to change. Ultimately these three scholars all deal with a socio-environmental change based on climate change as the reason for Norse Greenland's failure. In recent years they have teamed up to relay the latest data and form a more unified theory on the Norse Greenlanders' environment, lifestyle, and extinction.

In their 2012 publication they describe each North Atlantic island as having their own traditional ecological knowledge, or TEK. TEK is basically local knowledge of unique or specific environmental patterns that help determine when, where, or how to do something best for the best result. TEK is usually developed through several generations' experience working the land. Even the best way to manage a bad season is considered part of a culture's TEK.[88] The TEK model is not causation for the decline of Greenland, but rather an explanation for why and how the Norse adapted when conditions changed.

Recent isotope analysis and midden examinations indicate that approximately 40 percent of the Greenlanders' diet was made up of marine game, especially seals. During the early years of the Little Ice Age the percentage of their diet based on marine game grows to approximately eighty percent. The authors argue that "this shift represents an initially successful response to climate change and an initially resilient modification and intensification of sealing TEK by Greenlanders."[89] The Greenlanders apparently knew how to deal with years of bad weather and could find new resources. How they gathered the seals and other marine life is uncertain, although no evidence of the Norse adapting more effective methods of seal hunting has been found. These methods would include harpoons and Inuit-like clothing.[90]

However, the Norse did adapt to the best of their ability as opposed to many of the earlier theories described above. The conclusion of the 2012 article is that "the Norse Greenlanders were ultimately as much victims of conjunctures of global economic change, regional political change, culture contact, and major environmental change as the victims of any individual threat."[91] One of the only events the Greenlanders could control based on their TEK was the increase of marine hunting as a larger staple of their diets. Other events outside Greenland's control were not something the settlers could deal with.

Ultimately, this study mostly agrees with the concept that a combination of outside forces and internal problems were the culprits for the Norse demise in Greenland. The promised trade and contact with Norway was slow and infrequent, and European trade markets no longer required the resources offered by the North Atlantic environment, damaging economic and religious foundations in Greenland. The Icelanders were struggling to survive and adapt themselves, unable to offer any type of aid or assistance to Greenland. Iceland found a means to survive in cod fishing and then exporting it to the rest of Europe, while Greenland lost the ability to travel far enough into the ocean to catch cod or transport it to Europe.

The Greenlanders also failed to take full advantage of lumber resources in North America, a closer resource than Norway or England. Adaptability was possible, and the Norse Greenlanders did attempt to account for a deteriorating climate by using the sea more often. The Norse did fail to adapt completely, however, and were unwilling to learn from the thriving Inuit culture how to better improve fishing and marine hunting techniques. The Greenlanders also failed to find or develop better farming practices, such as the Icelanders practiced during the same period of bad weather. The Norse Greenlanders lived on the edge of survival and subsistence for nearly five hundred years, but failing to adapt completely to changing forces, both internal and external, caused them to lose the battle for survival.

NOTES

1. Henry S. Lucas, "Mediaeval Economic Relations between Flanders and Greenland," *Speculum* 12, no. 2 (April 1, 1937): 177, doi:10.2307/2849572.
2. Gwyn Jones, *The Norse Atlantic Saga: Being the Norse Voyages of Discovery and Settlement to Iceland, Greenland, and North America*, 2nd edition (New York: Oxford University Press, 1986), 86–87.
3. Poul Norlund, *Viking Settlers in Greenland and Their Descendants during Five Hundred Years* (New York: Kraus Reprint Co. History, 1971), 140–141.
4. Paul C Buckland, "The North Atlantic Environment," in *Vikings: The North Atlantic Saga*, ed. William W Fitzhugh and Elizabeth I Ward (Washington, D.C.: Smithsonian Institution Press, in association with the National Museum of Natural, 2000), 152.
5. Thomas H. McGovern et al., "Landscapes of Settlement in Northern Iceland: Historical Ecology of Human Impact and Climate Fluctuation on the Millennial Scale," *American Anthropologist* 109, no. 1 (2007): 29, doi:10.1525/aa.2007.109.1.27.
6. Buckland, "The North Atlantic Environment," 152.
7. McGovern et al., "Landscapes of Settlement in Northern Iceland," 39.
8. Richard Streeter, Andrew J. Dugmore, and Orri Vésteinsson, "Plague and Landscape Resilience in Premodern Iceland," *Proceedings of the National Academy of Sciences of the United States of America* 109, no. 10 (March 6, 2012): 3664–3665.
9. Jette Arneborg, "Greenland and Europe," in *Vikings: The North Atlantic Saga*, ed. William W Fitzhugh and Elizabeth I Ward (Washington, D.C.: Smithsonian Institution Press, in association with the National Museum of Natural History, 2000), 308.
10. Ibid., 309.
11. Christian Keller, "Vikings in the West Atlantic: A Model of Norse Greenlandic Medieval Society," in *The North Atlantic Frontier of Medieval Europe: Vikings and Celts*, ed. James Muldoon, vol. 3, The Expansion of Latin Europe, 1000-1500 (Surrey, England: Ashgate Publishing Limited, 2009), 41.
12. The most recent glaciovolcano to erupt was Iceland's Eyjafjallajökull, which famously erupted in spring of 2010 and interrupted European air traffic. The deadliest recent glaciovolcanic eruption was Nevado del Ruiz, located in the Columbian Andes and resulting in about 20,000 deaths. Alexandra Witze, "Fire & Ice: Volcanoes and Frozen Lands Make an Explosive Combo," *Science News* 178, no. 7 (July 25, 2010): 17.
13. Ibid., 16.
14. Jones, *The Norse Atlantic Saga*, 71.
15. Ibid.
16. Witze, "Fire & Ice: Volcanoes and Frozen Lands Make an Explosive Combo," 17.
17. Jones, *The Norse Atlantic Saga*, 71.
18. Sigurdur Thorarinsson, "Greetings from Iceland. Ash-Falls and Volcanic Aerosols in Scandinavia," *Geografiska Annaler. Series A, Physical Geography* 63, no. 3/4 (January 1, 1981): 110, doi:10.2307/520822.
19. Thomas Amorosi et al., "Raiding the Landscape: Human Impact in the Scandinavian North Atlantic," *Human Ecology* 25, no. 3 (September 1, 1997): 499.
20. Streeter, Dugmore, and Vésteinsson, "Plague and Landscape Resilience in Premodern Iceland," 3669; Buckland, "The North Atlantic Environment," 152.
21. Richard Hoffmann, "Frontier Foods for Late Medieval Consumers: Culture, Economy, Ecology," *Environment and History* 7, no. 2 (May 1, 2001): 149.
22. Ibid., 145.
23. Ibid., 144.
24. Ibid., 150.

25. Ivar Bárðarson, "A Fourteenth-Century Description of Greenland," trans. Derek Mathers, *Saga-Book* 33 (2009): 81.
26. Ibid.
27. Norlund, *Viking Settlers in Greenland and Their Descendants during Five Hundred Years*, 151.
28. Jones, *The Norse Atlantic Saga*, 262–267.
29. Dale Mackenzie Brown, "The Fate of Greenland's Vikings - Archaeology Magazine Archive," *Archaeology*, February 28, 2000, http://archive.archaeology.org/online/features/greenland/.
30. Ibid.
31. Kirsten A. Seaver, "Unanswered Questions," in *Vikings: The North Atlantic Saga*, ed. William W Fitzhugh and Elizabeth I Ward (Washington, D.C.: Smithsonian Institution Press, in association with the National Museum of Natural History, 2000), 278.
32. Vilhjalmur Stefansson, "The Icelandic Colony in Greenland," *American Anthropologist, New Series* 8, no. 2 (June 1906): 270.
33. Norlund, *Viking Settlers in Greenland and Their Descendants during Five Hundred Years*, 150.
34. Ibid., 149–150.
35. Ibid., 148.
36. Ibid.
37. Niels Lynnerup, "Life and Death in Norse Greenland," in *Vikings: The North Atlantic Saga*, ed. William W Fitzhugh and Elizabeth I Ward (Washington, D.C.: Smithsonian Institution Press, in association with the National Museum of Natural History, 2000), 290.
38. Thomas H. McGovern, "The Demise of Norse Greenland," in *Vikings: The North Atlantic Saga*, ed. William W Fitzhugh and Elizabeth I Ward (Washington, D.C.: Smithsonian Institution Press, in association with the National Museum of Natural History, 2000), 329–330.
39. Helge Ingstad, *Land Under the Pole Star: A Voyage to the Medieval Norse Settlements of Greenland and the Saga of a People That Vanished*, trans. Naomi Walford (New York: St. Martin's Press, 1966), 322.
40. Ibid.
41. Bárðarson, "A Fourteenth-Century Description of Greenland," 81.
42. Ingstad, *Land Under the Pole Star*, 323.
43. Oddvar K. Hoidal, "Norsemen and the North American Forests," *Journal of Forest History* 24, no. 4 (October 1980): 203.
44. Ingstad, *Land Under the Pole Star*, 324.
45. Ibid.
46. Birgitta Linderoth Wallace, "L'Anse Aux Meadows and Vinland: An Abandoned Experiment," in *Contact, Continuity, and Collapse: The Norse Colonization of the North Atlantic*, ed. James H Barrett (Turnhout, Belgium: Brepols, 2003), 226.
47. Ingstad, *Land Under the Pole Star*, 328.
48. Ibid., 326.
49. Ibid., 331.
50. Joel Berglund, "The Decline of the Norse Settlements in Greenland," *Arctic Anthropology* 23, no. 1/2 (January 1, 1986): 122.
51. Thomas H. McGovern, "The Archaeology of the Norse North Atlantic," *Annual Review of Anthropology* 19 (January 1, 1990): 341–342.
52. Amorosi et al., "Raiding the Landscape," 496.
53. Thomas H. McGovern et al., "Northern Islands, Human Error, and Environmental Degradation: A View of Social and Ecological Change in the Medieval North Atlantic," *Human Ecology* 16, no. 3 (September 1, 1988): 249.
54. Devin Powell, "Little Ice Age Began with Bang," *Science News* 181, no. 5 (March 10, 2012): 12.

55. C. J. Caseldine, "Neoglacial Glacier Variations in Northern Iceland: Examples from the Eyjafjördur Area," *Arctic and Alpine Research* 19, no. 3 (August 1, 1987): 296, doi:10.2307/1551365.

56. McGovern et al., "Northern Islands, Human Error, and Environmental Degradation," 248–250.

57. John A. Matthews and Keith R. Briffa, "The 'Little Ice Age': Re-Evaluation of an Evolving Concept," *Geografiska Annaler. Series A, Physical Geography* 87, no. 1 (January 1, 2005): 17; S. S. Visher, "Francois Emile Matthes, 1874-1948," *Annals of the Association of American Geographers* 38, no. 4 (December 1, 1948): 301.

58. G. J. Marcus, "The Greenland Trade-Route," *The Economic History Review*, New Series, 7, no. 1 (January 1, 1954): 78, doi:10.2307/2591227.

59. Ibid.

60. Ibid., 79–80; Norlund, *Viking Settlers in Greenland and Their Descendants during Five Hundred Years*, 103–104.

61. Finn Gad, *History of Greenland: I. Earliest Times to 1700*, trans. Ernst Dupont, First Canadian edition (McGill-Queen's University Press, 1971), 141.

62. Ibid., 142.

63. Ibid., 147.

64. Ibid., 151.

65. Ibid., 164.

66. Ibid., 155.

67. Ibid., 157.

68. Ibid., 162.

69. Ibid.

70. Lynnerup, "Life and Death in Norse Greenland," 288.

71. Hans Christian Gulløv, "The Nature of Contact between Native Greenlanders and Norse," *Journal of the North Atlantic*, July 1, 2008, 21–22, doi:10.3721/070425.

72. McGovern, "The Demise of Norse Greenland," 337.

73. Ibid.

74. Ibid.

75. Jette Arneborg, "Norse Greenland: Reflections on Settlement and Depopulation," in *Contact, Continuity, and Collapse: The Norse Colonization of the North Atlantic*, ed. James H Barrett (Turnhout, Belgium: Brepols, 2003), 176–177.

76. Ibid., 176.

77. Ibid., 177.

78. Ibid.; Arneborg, "Greenland and Europe," 316–317.

79. Berglund, "The Decline of the Norse Settlements in Greenland," 115.

80. Ibid., 125.

81. Ibid., 125–127.

82. Ibid., 118.

83. Bárðarson, "A Fourteenth-Century Description of Greenland," 81.

84. Joel Berglund, "The Farm Beneath the Sand," in *Vikings: The North Atlantic Saga*, ed. William W Fitzhugh and Elizabeth I Ward (Washington, D.C.: Smithsonian Institution Press, in association with the National Museum of Natural History, 2000), 303.

85. Ibid., 302.

86. Keller, "Vikings in the West Atlantic: A Model of Norse Greenlandic Medieval Society," 42.

87. Thomas H. McGovern, "Cows, Harp Seals, and Churchbells: Adaptation and Extinction in Norse Greenland," *Human Ecology* 8, no. 3 (September 1, 1980): 270.

88. Andrew J. Dugmore et al., "Cultural Adaptation, Compounding Vulnerabilities and Conjunctures in Norse Greenland," *Proceedings of the National Academy of Sciences* 109, no. 10 (March 6, 2012): 3660, doi:10.1073/pnas.1115292109.

89. Ibid., 3661.

90. Thomas H. McGovern, "Climate, Correlation, and Causation in Norse Greenland," *Arctic Anthropology* 28, no. 2 (January 1, 1991): 91.

91. Dugmore et al., "Cultural Adaptation, Compounding Vulnerabilities and Conjunctures in Norse Greenland," 3662.

SIX
Conclusion

Scandinavia expanded rapidly during the Viking Age, resulting in the Norse settlement of Iceland and Greenland. As people began settling the new lands in the North Atlantic they also tried constructing ideal societies based on experiences in their homelands. Greenlanders and Icelanders faced unique circumstances and were forced to adopt lifestyles and livelihoods in order to survive. In the face of climate change and rapidly shifting economies, Iceland survived and Greenland failed.

The available medieval sources are sparse regarding Iceland and nearly non-existent regarding Greenland. The main source for most historians is the collection of stories known as Icelandic sagas, many with unknown authors that teeter on the edge of fictional and fanciful. However, the interpretation of the sagas has greatly advanced in recent decades, allowing researchers to better understand the settings and historical aspects of the sagas that are accurate and useful. Ongoing historical and archaeological research continues to provide evidence supporting the sagas as mostly true and accurate accounts of the time periods they describe.

From the early *landnám* periods in both Iceland and Greenland the civilizations were based mainly on agriculture and animal husbandry. Many of the original settlers in Iceland are described in *Landnámabók*, although Erik the Red and his initial settlement of Greenland is also included.[1] The earliest settlers claimed large areas of land and divided that land amongst followers and friends. Despite early settlers' claims on large parcels of land, political and social power was fluid in both islands, with a number of people holding the *goðar* status throughout Iceland and Greenland.

Because power changed hands relatively easily the residents relied on the Althing system to maintain order and justice, even after submitting to Norway's kings. The *goðar* were responsible for controlling order and handling feuds in their local areas, but they also had to maintain the loyalty of local *bændr*, or free farmers. The *bændr* had the responsibility of supporting their *goðar* and attending the Things. Through this system, the Icelanders and Greenlanders successfully maintained society until the will of Norway's king combined with power consolidated in the hands of only a few families and propelled treaties of submission in the 1260s.

The Thing system also changed Iceland to a Christian country around the year 1000, avoiding civil war. The Icelanders' adoption of Christianity at the Althing is a rare example of a religious conversion that was willingly accepted without violence. It also signified the desire of the Icelanders to remain independent from European kings hoping to claim responsibility for their conversion, which would have provided the monarchs with more power and influence over Iceland.

Some monarchs did hold power and some control over Iceland and Greenland, particularly the kings of Norway. Since many of the settlers across the North Atlantic islands were of Norwegian families, the Norwegian crown was regularly involved in their affairs. The settlers remained rather defiant of Norway's authority, even safeguarding many of the rights they claimed to be ancestral during the *Gizurarsáttmáli*, the 1262 Althing decision when Iceland began submitting to Norway.[2]

Newly introduced Christianity also played a role in altering society in both countries. Church structure imitated the feudal ranks and was dependent upon power in the hands of a few rather than many, complementing the consolidation of power that takes place in thirteenth century Iceland. *Goðar* utilized the construction of small churches on their landholdings or on donated land as another way to sustain their family for future generations through their ability to withhold a portion of the tithe. The construction of private churches helped stabilize *goðar-bændr* relationships because the *goðar* were then responsible for providing a means to religion and worship.

Iceland and Greenland also joined the extensive trade networks of the Viking Age. Residents of both countries are known to have traveled and traded throughout Europe, the Mediterranean region, and even western parts of Asia. Trade and contact slowly decreased, especially in Greenland, forcing both countries to be dependent on Norway for continued trade opportunities. Greenlanders also explored North America shortly after 1000, initiating the first European contact with the Americas nearly five centuries before Columbus' voyages. Historians still debate the importance and the impact of this contact, but North America provided valuable resources for the Norse Greenlanders. The region of Markland had the ability to be a source of necessary lumber supplies for Greenland, but it does not appear to be fully exploited. In spite of increased research and archaeological work, the Norse presence in North America is still a relatively young topic with much more to be explored and explained.

The greatest mystery, however, is the extinction of Norse Greenland in the fifteenth century. Early theories tried to find a single cause for the destruction and death of the Norse inhabitants of Greenland. The major theories included destruction by pirates and attacks by Inuit, as well as leaving the settlements behind and intermarrying with the Inuit, or even a mass exodus to North America. Recent scholarship addresses the issue from multiple points. Climate change is a major cause for what finally pushed the Greenlanders past sustainable farming practices, but adaptation practices and socioeconomic changes created an unmanageable situation.

The final causes for the failure of Norse Greenland was a long-term decline of the different topics discussed in this study, specifically agriculture and animal husbandry practices, trade and contact with Norway as well as the rest of Europe, and social organization and power structures. Iceland was unable to help the Greenlanders because Iceland was suffering through its own set of problems, including its own loss of farmland and trade resources, as well as an increase in devastating volcanic activity. The loss of the northern hunting grounds, *Norðrestur*, was also devastating to Greenland as it eliminated both a regular food source and products that attracted European merchants. Climate change helped accelerate the decline of certain traits, such as trade and agriculture patterns, but some things were also declining since the early settlers arrived. Soil erosion was imminent in Greenland due to the extensive grazing and farming practices that eliminated plants and small trees which held the soil in place. The Little Ice Age forced Greenlanders to adapt to the worsening climate, but the adaptations were only successful for a short while and were not sustainable.

A comparison of the Norse settlements of Greenland and Iceland provide scholars with the opportunity to study two similar yet unique societies—one that failed and one that survived. Medieval Iceland offers insights into how societies develop from independent settlers and farmers to interdependent groups capable of creating a national assembly. Medieval Greenland provides an awareness for what happens when societies attempt to replicate another country's model without accounting for the differences in environments and social structures. Greenland also warns of the dangers of living on the edge of subsistence levels and failing to quickly and adequately adapt to changes impacting subsistence techniques.

The Norse settlements in the North Atlantic have been mostly ignored or disregarded by scholars focusing on frontiers in the Middle Ages. Medieval frontier studies devote substantial time to conflicted borders and the militarization of states, two things neither Greenland nor Iceland had to manage.[3] Settlers in Iceland and Greenland had no other population to contend with when creating their societies. The Norse could attempt to create their idealized societies, and historians have the opportunity to understand a society based on agricultural and animal husbandry with little outside influence.

Religion plays an important role in every study of frontier societies—whether as a guidepost or as a cause for conflict. The role of religion and the changes brought by Christianity to both Iceland and Greenland play vital roles in the history and development of their respective countries, with Iceland being nearly on the brink of civil war because of religion. It could be argued that the role of Christianity in Greenland is deserving of its own dedicated study because so little is known and understood about it. While the role of religion to the Greenlanders themselves is becoming better understood, the role and actual importance of the Church is still uncertain, in part due to the long absences of bishops and church officials.

The discoveries of Iceland and Greenland were not the end of the expansion of the Norse across the North Atlantic, nor did the settlers in the North Atlantic islands try to avoid involvement in European affairs. The evidence suggests that Greenlanders and Icelanders alike traveled throughout Europe and western Asia on peaceful trade missions and for war. From Greenland the Norse continued to travel west, eventually landing and exploring parts of North America. While the Norse settlement of America was short, the impact was far reaching. The Greenlanders obtained valuable resources and continued to do so presumably until Greenland ceased to exist. Even more important, which the Smithsonian's William Fitzhugh describes the best, is "the familiarity Native Americans gained about European habits, behavior, and materials which helped them take best advantage of future interactions."[4]

The Norse expansion across the North Atlantic altered the landscape of Europe. Not only were new lands discovered, but new people too. The societies in Iceland and Greenland represented the idealized versions of societies without kings or queens, although their survival depended on connections with those kingdoms. Greenland was unable to adapt to changing environmental and economic conditions, while the Icelanders changed their grazing patterns and relied on a fishing economy in order to survive their changing conditions. Recognizing and studying those changes and the impact those changes had on their societies allows historians to better understand the way new frontier societies develop and cope. The growing evidence and artifacts from Norse Iceland and Greenland can teach scholars as much about how civilizations grow as well as why some fail.

NOTES

1. Ari Thorgilsson, *Landnámabók: The Book of Settlements*, trans. Paul Edwards and Hermann Pálsson (Winnipeg, Man.: University of Manitoba Press, 2006).

2. Patricia Pires Boulhosa, *Icelanders and the Kings of Norway: Mediaeval Sagas and Legal Texts* (Leiden: Brill Academic Pub, 2005), 87.

3. J. R. S. Phillips, *The Medieval Expansion of Europe* (New York: Oxford University Press, 1988), vi-vii; Robert Bartlett and Angus MacKay, *Medieval Frontier Societies*, Reprint (New York: Oxford University Press, 2011), v-vi.

4. William W Fitzhugh, "Puffins, Ringed Pins, and Runestones: The Viking Passage to America," in *Vikings: The North Atlantic Saga*, ed. William W Fitzhugh and Elizabeth I Ward (Washington, D.C.: Smithsonian Institution Press, in association with the National Museum of Natural History, 2000), 24.

Bibliography

Adam of Bremen. *History of the Archbishops of Hamburg-Bremen*. Translated by Francis Joseph Tschan and Timothy Reuter. New York: Columbia University Press, 2002.
Addleshaw, G.W.O. *The Pastoral Structure of the Celtic Church in Northern Britain*. York, England: St. Anthony's Press, 1973.
Amorosi, Thomas, Paul Buckland, Andrew Dugmore, Jon H. Ingimundarson, and Thomas H. McGovern. "Raiding the Landscape: Human Impact in the Scandinavian North Atlantic." *Human Ecology* 25, no. 3 (September 1, 1997): 491–518.
Andersson, Theodore M. "The King of Iceland." *Speculum* 74, no. 4 (October 1, 1999): 923–34. doi:10.2307/2886968.
Arneborg, Jette. "Greenland and Europe." In *Vikings: The North Atlantic Saga*, edited by William W Fitzhugh and Elizabeth I Ward, 304–17. Washington, D.C.: Smithsonian Institution Press, in association with the National Museum of Natural History, 2000.
———. "Norse Greenland: Reflections on Settlement and Depopulation." In *Contact, Continuity, and Collapse: The Norse Colonization of the North Atlantic*, edited by James H Barrett, 163–81. Turnhout, Belgium: Brepols, 2003.
Attwood, Katrina C., trans. "The Saga of Gunnlaug Serpent-Tongue." In *The Sagas of Icelanders: A Selection*, 558–94. New York: Penguin Books, 2001.
Bárðarson, Ivar. "A Fourteenth-Century Description of Greenland." Translated by Derek Mathers. *Saga-Book* 33 (2009): 78–82.
Barrett, James H. "Introduction." In *Contact, Continuity, and Collapse: The Norse Colonization of the North Atlantic*, edited by James H Barrett, 1–5. Turnhout, Belgium: Brepols, 2008.
Bartlett, Robert, and Angus MacKay. *Medieval Frontier Societies*. Reprint. New York: Oxford University Press, 2011.
Berglund, Joel. "The Decline of the Norse Settlements in Greenland." *Arctic Anthropology* 23, no. 1/2 (January 1, 1986): 109–35.
———. "The Farm Beneath the Sand." In *Vikings: The North Atlantic Saga*, edited by William W Fitzhugh and Elizabeth I Ward, 295–303. Washington, D.C.: Smithsonian Institution Press, in association with the National Museum of Natural History, 2000.
Boulhosa, Patricia Pires. *Icelanders and the Kings of Norway: Mediaeval Sagas and Legal Texts*. Leiden: Brill Academic Pub, 2005.
Brannon, Patrick V. "Medieval Ireland: Music in Cathedral, Church and Cloister." *Early Music* 28, no. 2 (May 1, 2000): 193–202.
Bregaint, David. "Conquering Minds: Konungs Skuggsia and the Annexation of Iceland in the Thirteenth Century." *Scandinavian Studies* 84, no. 4 (2012): 439–66.
Brown, Dale Mackenzie. "The Fate of Greenland's Vikings - Archaeology Magazine Archive." *Archaeology*, February 28, 2000. http://archive.archaeology.org/online/features/greenland/.
Brun, Eske. "Greenland." *Arctic* 19, no. 1 (March 1, 1966): 62–69.
Buckland, Paul C. "The North Atlantic Environment." In *Vikings: The North Atlantic Saga*, edited by William W Fitzhugh and Elizabeth I Ward, 146–53. Washington, D.C.: Smithsonian Institution Press, in association with the National Museum of Natural History, 2000.
Burns, Robert I. "The Significance of the Frontier in the Middle Ages." In *Medieval Frontier Societies*, edited by Robert Bartlett and Angus MacKay, Reprint., 307–30. New York: Oxford University Press, 2011.

Byock, Jesse L. *Medieval Iceland: Society, Sagas, and Power*. Berkeley: University of California Press, 1988.

———. "Saga Form, Oral Prehistory, and the Icelandic Social Context." *New Literary History* 16, no. 1 (Autumn 1984): 153–73.

———. *Viking Age Iceland*. New York: Penguin Books, 2001.

Caseldine, C. J. "Neoglacial Glacier Variations in Northern Iceland: Examples from the Eyjafjördur Area." *Arctic and Alpine Research* 19, no. 3 (August 1, 1987): 296–304. doi:10.2307/1551365.

Cook, Robert, trans. *Njal's Saga*. New York: Penguin Classics, 2001.

Cox, Steven L. "A Norse Penny from Maine." In *Vikings: The North Atlantic Saga*, edited by William W Fitzhugh and Elizabeth I Ward, 206–7. Washington, D.C.: Smithsonian Institution Press, in association with the National Museum of Natural History, 2000.

Dicuil. "Liber de Mensura Orbis Terrae." In *The Viking Age: A Reader*, edited by Angus A. Somerville and R. Andrew McDonald, translated by J.J. Tierney, 330–31. Toronto: University of Toronto Press, 2010.

Dugmore, Andrew J., Christian Keller, and Thomas H. McGovern. "Norse Greenland Settlement: Reflections on Climate Change, Trade, and the Contrasting Fates of Human Settlements in the North Atlantic Islands." *Arctic Anthropology* 44, no. 1 (January 1, 2007): 12–36.

Dugmore, Andrew J., Thomas H. McGovern, Orri Vésteinsson, Jette Arneborg, Richard Streeter, and Christian Keller. "Cultural Adaptation, Compounding Vulnerabilities and Conjunctures in Norse Greenland." *Proceedings of the National Academy of Sciences* 109, no. 10 (March 6, 2012): 3658–63. doi:10.1073/pnas.1115292109.

"Earth Snapshot—Eyjafjörður, Central Northern Iceland's Longest Fjord." Accessed December 29, 2014. http://www.eosnap.com/snapshots/eyjafjor%C3%B0ur-central-northern-icelands-longest-fjord/.

Enterline, James Robert. *Erikson, Eskimos, and Columbus: Medieval European Knowledge of America*. Baltimore: Johns Hopkins University Press, 2004.

———. *Viking America: The Norse Crossings & Their Legacy*. Garden City, N.Y: J. R. Enterline, 1972.

Fitzhugh, William W. "Puffins, Ringed Pins, and Runestones: The Viking Passage to America." In *Vikings: The North Atlantic Saga*, edited by William W Fitzhugh and Elizabeth I Ward, 11–25. Washington, D.C.: Smithsonian Institution Press, in association with the National Museum of Natural History, 2000.

Fitzhugh, William W, and Elizabeth I Ward. "Celebrating the Viking Past: A Viking Millennium in America." In *Vikings: The North Atlantic Saga*, edited by William W Fitzhugh and Elizabeth I Ward, 351–53. Washington, D.C.: Smithsonian Institution Press, in association with the National Museum of Natural History, 2000.

Fitzhugh, William W, Ward, and National Museum of Natural History (U.S.). *Vikings: The North Atlantic Saga*. Washington: Smithsonian Institution Press, in association with the National Museum of Natural History, 2000.

Gad, Finn. *History of Greenland: I. Earliest Times to 1700*. Translated by Ernst Dupont. First Canadian edition. McGill-Queen's University Press, 1971.

Gorman, Jessica. "Questions of Origin." *Science News* 162, no. 7 (August 17, 2002): 109. doi:10.2307/4013794.

Gräslund, Anne-Sofie. "Religion, Art, and Runes." In *Vikings: The North Atlantic Saga*, edited by William W Fitzhugh and Elizabeth I Ward, 55–69. Washington, D.C.: Smithsonian Institution Press, in association with the National Museum of Natural History, 2000.

Guðmundsson, Guðmundur J. "Greenland and the Wider World." *Journal of the North Atlantic* 2, no. sp2 (January 1, 2009): 66–73. doi:10.3721/037.002.s208.

Gulløv, Hans Christian. "The Nature of Contact between Native Greenlanders and Norse." *Journal of the North Atlantic*, July 1, 2008, 16–24. doi:10.3721/070425.

Gunnel, Terry, trans. "The Saga of Hrafnkel Frey's Godi." In *The Sagas of Icelanders: A Selection*, 436–62. New York: Penguin Books, 2001.

Gunnel, Terry, trans. "The Tale of Halldor Snorrason II." In *The Sagas of Icelanders: A Selection*, 685–93. New York: Penguin Classics, 2001.

Hanson, R. P. C. "The Reaction of the Church to the Collapse of the Western Roman Empire in the Fifth Century." *Vigiliae Christianae* 26, no. 4 (December 1, 1972): 272–87. doi:10.2307/1583559.

Hastrup, Kristen. *Culture and History in Medieval Iceland: An Anthropological Analysis of Structure and Change*. Oxford ; New York: Oxford University Press, 1985.

Hedeager, Lotte. "From Warrior to Trade Economy." In *Vikings: The North Atlantic Saga*, edited by William W Fitzhugh and Elizabeth I Ward, 84–85. Washington, D.C.: Smithsonian Institution Press, in association with the National Museum of Natural History, 2000.

Hoffmann, Richard. "Frontier Foods for Late Medieval Consumers: Culture, Economy, Ecology." *Environment and History* 7, no. 2 (May 1, 2001): 131–67.

Hoidal, Oddvar K. "Norsemen and the North American Forests." *Journal of Forest History* 24, no. 4 (October 1980): 200–203.

Imer, Lisbeth M. "The Runic Inscriptions from Vatnahverfi and the Evidence of Communication." *Journal of the North Atlantic* 2, no. sp2 (January 1, 2009): 74–81. doi:10.3721/037.002.s209.

Ingstad, Helge. *Land Under the Pole Star: A Voyage to the Medieval Norse Settlements of Greenland and the Saga of a People That Vanished*. Translated by Naomi Walford. New York: St. Martin's Press, 1966.

Jesch, Judith. *Women in the Viking Age*. Woodbridge, Suffolk: Boydell Press, 1991.

Jochens, Jenny. "Late and Peaceful: Iceland's Conversion Through Arbitration in 1000." *Speculum* 74, no. 3 (July 1, 1999): 621–55. doi:10.2307/2886763.

Jones, Gwyn. *The Norse Atlantic Saga: Being the Norse Voyages of Discovery and Settlement to Iceland, Greenland, and North America*. 2nd edition. New York: Oxford University Press, 1986.

Jorgensen, Lars. "Political Organization and Social Life." In *Vikings: The North Atlantic Saga*, edited by William W Fitzhugh and Elizabeth I Ward, 72–83. Washington, D.C.: Smithsonian Institution Press, in association with the National Museum of Natural History, 2000.

Kaland, Sigrid H.H., and Irmelin Martens. "Farming and Daily Life." In *Vikings: The North Atlantic Saga*, edited by William W Fitzhugh and Elizabeth I Ward, 42–54. Washington, D.C.: Smithsonian Institution Press, in association with the National Museum of Natural History, 2000.

Keller, Christian. "Vikings in the West Atlantic: A Model of Norse Greenlandic Medieval Society." In *The North Atlantic Frontier of Medieval Europe: Vikings and Celts*, edited by James Muldoon, 3:25–46. The Expansion of Latin Europe, 1000-1500. Surrey, England: Ashgate Publishing Limited, 2009.

Kolodny, Annette. *In Search of First Contact: The Vikings of Vinland, the Peoples of the Dawnland, and the Anglo-American Anxiety of Discovery*. Durham, NC: Duke University Press Books, 2012.

Krappe, Alexander Haggerty. "The Valkyrie Episode in the Njals Saga." *Modern Language Notes* 43, no. 7 (November 1928): 471–74.

Kunz, Keneva, trans. "Eirik the Red's Saga." In *The Sagas of Icelanders: A Selection*, 653–76. New York: Penguin Books, 2001.

———. "The Saga of the Greenlanders." In *The Sagas of Icelanders: A Selection*, 636–52. New York: Penguin Books, 2001.

———. "The Saga of the People of Laxardal." In *The Sagas of Icelanders: A Selection*, 270–421. New York: Penguin Books, 2001.

Lucas, Henry S. "Mediaeval Economic Relations between Flanders and Greenland." *Speculum* 12, no. 2 (April 1, 1937): 167–81. doi:10.2307/2849572.

Lund, Niels. "The Danish Empire and the End of the Viking Age." In *The Oxford Illustrated History of the Vikings*, edited by Peter Sawyer, 156–81. Oxford: Oxford University Press, 2001.

Lynnerup, Niels. "Life and Death in Norse Greenland." In *Vikings: The North Atlantic Saga*, edited by William W Fitzhugh and Elizabeth I Ward, 285–94. Washington, D.C.: Smithsonian Institution Press, in association with the National Museum of Natural History, 2000.

Marcus, G. J. "The Greenland Trade-Route." *The Economic History Review*, New Series, 7, no. 1 (January 1, 1954): 71–80. doi:10.2307/2591227.

———. "The Norse Traffic with Iceland." *The Economic History Review*, New Series, 9, no. 3 (January 1, 1957): 408–19. doi:10.2307/2591132.

Matthews, John A., and Keith R. Briffa. "The 'Little Ice Age': Re-Evaluation of an Evolving Concept." *Geografiska Annaler. Series A, Physical Geography* 87, no. 1 (January 1, 2005): 17–36.

Maxwell, Anthony, trans. "The Tale of Audun from the West Fjords." In *The Sagas of Icelanders: A Selection*, 717–22. New York: Penguin Classics, 2000.

Maxwell, Anthony, trans. "The Tale of Thorstein Staff-Struck." In *The Sagas of Icelanders: A Selection*, 677–84. New York: Penguin Classics, 2001.

McGovern, Thomas H. "Climate, Correlation, and Causation in Norse Greenland." *Arctic Anthropology* 28, no. 2 (January 1, 1991): 77–100.

———. "Cows, Harp Seals, and Churchbells: Adaptation and Extinction in Norse Greenland." *Human Ecology* 8, no. 3 (September 1, 1980): 245–75.

———. "The Archaeology of the Norse North Atlantic." *Annual Review of Anthropology* 19 (January 1, 1990): 331–51.

———. "The Demise of Norse Greenland." In *Vikings: The North Atlantic Saga*, edited by William W Fitzhugh and Elizabeth I Ward, 327–39. Washington, D.C.: Smithsonian Institution Press, in association with the National Museum of Natural History, 2000.

McGovern, Thomas H., Gerald Bigelow, Thomas Amorosi, and Daniel Russell. "Northern Islands, Human Error, and Environmental Degradation: A View of Social and Ecological Change in the Medieval North Atlantic." *Human Ecology* 16, no. 3 (September 1, 1988): 225–70.

McGovern, Thomas H., Orri Vésteinsson, Adolf Fridriksson, Mike Church, Ian Lawson, Ian A. Simpson, Arni Einarsson, et al. "Landscapes of Settlement in Northern Iceland: Historical Ecology of Human Impact and Climate Fluctuation on the Millennial Scale." *American Anthropologist* 109, no. 1 (2007): 27–51. doi:10.1525/aa.2007.109.1.27.

McKusick, Marshall, and Erik Wahlgren. "The Norse Penny Mystery." *Archaeology of Eastern North America* 8 (Fall 1980): 1–10.

Meinberg, Carl H. "The Norse Church in Medieval America." *The Catholic Historical Review* 11, no. 2 (July 1, 1925): 179–216.

Miller, William Ian. *Bloodtaking and Peacemaking: Feud, Law, and Society in Saga Iceland*. Chicago: University Of Chicago Press, 1997.

Morris, Christopher D. "The Viking Age in Europe." In *Vikings: The North Atlantic Saga*, edited by William W Fitzhugh and Elizabeth I Ward, 99–102. Washington, D.C.: Smithsonian Institution Press, in association with the National Museum of Natural History, 2000.

Muldoon, James. "Introduction." In *The North Atlantic Frontier of Medieval Europe: Vikings and Celts*, edited by James Muldoon, xiii – xxxvii. Farnham, England: Ashgate, 2009.

———. *The North Atlantic Frontier of Medieval Europe: Vikings and Celts*. Farnham, England: Ashgate, 2009.

"NABO: North Atlantic Biocultural Organisation." Accessed April 7, 2014. http://www.nabohome.org/.

Norlund, Poul. *Viking Settlers in Greenland and Their Descendants during Five Hundred Years*. New York: Kraus Reprint Co., 1971.

Olafsson, Haraldur. "Sagas of Western Expansion." In *Vikings: The North Atlantic Saga*, edited by William W Fitzhugh and Elizabeth I Ward, 142–45. Washington, D.C.:

Smithsonian Institution Press, in association with the National Museum of Natural History, 2000.
Ordower, Henry. "Exploring the Literary Function of Law and Litigation in 'Njal's Saga.'" *Cardozo Studies in Law and Literature* 3, no. 1 (April 1991): 41–61. doi:10.2307/743501.
Parks Canada Agency, Government of Canada. "Parks Canada—L'Anse Aux Meadows National Historic Site - History," September 20, 2012. http://www.pc.gc.ca/eng/lhn-nhs/nl/meadows/natcul.aspx.
Patterson, William P., Kristin A. Dietrich, Chris Holmden, John T. Andrews, and Darren Grocke. "Two Millennia of North Atlantic Seasonality and Implications for Norse Colonies." *Proceedings of the National Academy of Sciences of the United States of America* 107, no. 12 (March 23, 2010): 5306–10.
Paulsen, Caroline, Mike Church, Ian Simpson, Paul Adderley, Albina Palsdottir, and Thomas H. McGovern. *Archaeological Excavations at Qassiarsuk 2005-2006: Field Report (Data Structure Report)*. Bolungarvik, Iceland: North Atlantic Biocultural Organization, April 2007.
Phillips, J. R. S. *The Medieval Expansion of Europe*. New York: Oxford University Press, 1988.
Powell, Devin. "Little Ice Age Began with Bang." *Science News* 181, no. 5 (March 10, 2012): 12.
Rafnsson, Sveinbjorn. "The Atlantic Islands." In *The Oxford Illustrated History of the Vikings*, edited by Peter Sawyer, 110–33. Oxford: Oxford University Press, 2001.
Regal, Martin S. "Gisli Sursson's Saga." In *The Sagas of Icelanders: A Selection*, 496–557. New York: Penguin Books, 2001.
Roesdahl, Else. *The Vikings*. New York: Penguin Books, 1998.
Sawyer, Birgit, and Peter Sawyer. *Medieval Scandinavia: From Conversion to Reformation, circa 800-1500*. Minneapolis: University of Minnesota Press, 1993.
Scudder, Bernard, trans. "Egil's Sagas." In *The Sagas of Icelanders: A Selection*, 3–184. New York: Penguin Books, 2001.
Seaver, Kirsten A. "Unanswered Questions." In *Vikings: The North Atlantic Saga*, edited by William W Fitzhugh and Elizabeth I Ward, 270–79. Washington, D.C.: Smithsonian Institution Press, in association with the National Museum of Natural History, 2000.
Sigurðsson, Gisli. "Eddas and Sagas in Medieval Iceland." In *Vikings: The North Atlantic Saga*, edited by William W Fitzhugh and Elizabeth I Ward, 186–87. Washington, D.C.: Smithsonian Institution Press, in association with the National Museum of Natural History, 2000.
Sigurðsson, Jon Viðar. *Chieftains and Power in the Icelandic Commonwealth*. Odense: University Press of Southern Denmark, 1999.
Somerville, Angus A., and R. Andrew McDonald, eds. "The Saga of Eirik the Red." In *The Viking Age: A Reader*, 419–21. Toronto: University of Toronto Press, 2010.
Sorensen, Preben Meulengracht. "Religions Old and New." In *The Oxford Illustrated History of the Vikings*, edited by Peter Sawyer, 202–24. Oxford: Oxford University Press, 2001.
Stefansson, Vilhjalmur. "The Icelandic Colony in Greenland." *American Anthropologist, New Series* 8, no. 2 (June 1906): 262–70.
Streeter, Richard, Andrew J. Dugmore, and Orri Vésteinsson. "Plague and Landscape Resilience in Premodern Iceland." *Proceedings of the National Academy of Sciences of the United States of America* 109, no. 10 (March 6, 2012): 3664–69.
Sturluson, Snorri. "Harald Sigurdarson's Saga." In *The Viking Age: A Reader*, edited and translated by Angus A. Somerville and R. Andrew McDonald, 321–25. Toronto: University of Toronto Press, 2010.
Sutherland, Patricia D. "The Norse and the Native Americans." In *Vikings: The North Atlantic Saga*, edited by William W Fitzhugh and Elizabeth I Ward, 238–47. Washington, D.C.: Smithsonian Institution Press, in association with the National Museum of Natural History, 2000.

Tedesco, M., J.E. Box, J. Cappelen, X. Fettweis, T. Mote, R.S.W. Van de Wal, C.J.P.P. Smeets, and J. Wahr. "Arctic Report Card - Greenland Ice Sheet." *Arctic Report Card*, January 27, 2015. http://www.arctic.noaa.gov/reportcard/greenland_ice_sheet.html.

Thorarinsson, Sigurdur. "Greetings from Iceland. Ash-Falls and Volcanic Aerosols in Scandinavia." *Geografiska Annaler. Series A, Physical Geography* 63, no. 3/4 (January 1, 1981): 109–18. doi:10.2307/520822.

Thorgilsson, Ari. "Íslendingabók." In *The Viking Age: A Reader*, edited by Angus A. Somerville and R. Andrew McDonald, 346, 417–19. Toronto: University of Toronto Press, 2010.

———. *Landnámabók: The Book of Settlements*. Translated by Paul Edwards and Hermann Pálsson. Winnipeg, Man.: University of Manitoba Press, 2006.

Thorlaksson, Helgi. "The Icelandic Commonwealth Period: Building a New Society." In *Vikings: The North Atlantic Saga*, edited by William W Fitzhugh and Elizabeth I Ward, 175–85. Washington, D.C.: Smithsonian Institution Press, in association with the National Museum of Natural History, 2000.

Vésteinsson, O., M. J. Church, A. J. Dugmore, T. H. McGovern, and A. J. Newton. "Expensive Errors or Rational Choices : The Pioneer Fringe in Late Viking Age Iceland." *European Journal of Post-Classical Archaeologies* 4 (May 1, 2014): 39–68.

Vésteinsson, Orri. "Parishes and Communities in Norse Greenland." *Journal of the North Atlantic* 2, no. sp2 (January 1, 2009): 138–50. doi:10.3721/037.002.s215.

———. "The Archaeology of Landnam: Early Settlement in Iceland." In *Vikings: The North Atlantic Saga*, edited by William W Fitzhugh and Elizabeth I Ward, 164–74. Washington, D.C.: Smithsonian Institution Press, in association with the National Museum of Natural History, 2000.

———. *The Christianization of Iceland: Priests, Power, and Social Change 1000-1300*. Oxford: Oxford University Press, 2000.

Visher, S. S. "Francois Emile Matthes, 1874-1948." *Annals of the Association of American Geographers* 38, no. 4 (December 1, 1948): 301–4.

Wallace, Birgitta Linderoth. "L'Anse Aux Meadows and Vinland: An Abandoned Experiment." In *Contact, Continuity, and Collapse: The Norse Colonization of the North Atlantic*, edited by James H Barrett, 207–38. Turnhout, Belgium: Brepols, 2003.

Winroth, Anders. *Conversion of Scandinavia: Vikings, Merchants, and Missionaries in the Remaking of Northern Europe*. New Haven, CT: Yale University Press, 2014.

Witze, Alexandra. "Fire & Ice: Volcanoes and Frozen Lands Make an Explosive Combo." *Science News* 178, no. 7 (July 25, 2010): 16–20.

Index

Adam of Bremen, 45, 48, 51, 65
Adrian II, pope, 20
Africa, 7, 69
agriculture, 2, 31–32, 60, 74–75, 82–84, 93–94
Althing, 40–42, 43, 46, 53, 91–92
archaeology, 6, 13, 79
archbishop, 45, 48, 50, 51
Arctic Circle, 19, 27, 75
Ari the Learned, 20–22, 25, 27–28, 29, 46–47, 48
Asia, 1, 7; travels to, 59, 63, 92, 94
assembly. *See* Thing
Atlantic Ocean. *See* North Atlantic
Aud the Deep Minded, 21–22

Baltic, 59
basque, 68, 81
Bárðarson, Ivar, 5, 41, 73, 73–80, 75, 83
Birka, 59
bishop, 10, 37, 40, 41, 48–49, 51, 75, 76, 84, 94
Black Death, 53, 73, 80
bóndi (bændr, pl.), 13, 38–42, 91–92
Brattahlid, 29, 37, 40–41
British Isles, 59

Canada, 3, 8, 11, 68. *See also* North America
cattle, 30–31, 66, 80, 84
Celtic, 4, 10, 48–49, 61
Charlemagne, emperor, 1
chieftain, 1, 9, 10, 23, 24, 26, 42, 52, 53, 76; power, 13, 22–23, 82; system, 2, 10, 13, 28, 32, 37, 38–39, 44, 49, 52
Christ, 9, 45, 46
Christian: person, 47, 47–48, 49, 76; religion, 10, 20, 44, 45, 45–46, 47, 48, 63, 66, 92

Christianity, 22, 48, 54, 61, 63, 94; blends with Norse mythology, 9, 44, 46, 50, 66; Celtic Christians, 48–49; conversion to. *See* conversion; development, 9; importance, 4, 9, 10, 41, 44–45, 49, 92
church: buildings and lands, 5, 51, 75–76; the Church, 10, 50, 52, 84, 94; Irish Catholic Church, 10, 48–49; officials, 5, 38, 75, 94; role of, 9, 10–11, 12, 13, 14, 44, 46–47, 50, 92; Roman Catholic Church, 10, 48–49, 84
climate change, 2, 6, 12, 75, 77, 79–81, 82, 84–85, 91; Little Ice Age, 73, 74, 79–80, 84–85, 93; Medieval Warm Period, 19–20, 74, 79–80
cod, 30, 75, 85
Columbus, Christopher, 2, 63, 65, 92
Commonwealth, 2, 3, 13, 37, 53
Constantinople, 63, 64
conversion, 2, 8, 9–11, 37, 38, 43–47, 48–49, 51, 54, 60, 92
cow, 26, 30–31, 62, 75, 78, 83. *See also* cattle
cult, 10

Denmark, 1, 13, 20, 22, 45–46, 47, 49, 50, 62, 62–63, 63, 73, 79
domestic animals. *See* livestock
Dorset culture, 27–28, 32

Eastern Settlement, 29–30, 49, 78–79, 83
emigrate, 23
emigration, 24, 78, 82
England and the English, 24, 75, 76, 79
environment, 2, 13, 14, 20, 75, 79, 84, 85. *See also* climate change
Erik the Red, 27–29, 32, 40, 41, 47–48, 91

Eriksfjord, 29
Ethelred II (Æthelred II), king of England, 44–45, 61
Europe and Europeans, 1, 14, 22, 24–25, 25, 26, 28, 39, 46, 49, 50, 51, 53, 65, 73, 75, 76, 77, 92; contact with, 2, 10, 19, 59–60, 61, 62, 63, 70, 74, 82, 85, 92, 93, 94; continental, 1, 10, 48, 49, 51, 59, 61–62, 63, 69; Eastern, 59; expansion, 1, 7, 7–9, 64, 65, 69, 94; Northern, 4, 24, 44; Western, 1

Farm Beneath the Sand, archaeological site, 12, 31, 60, 83
Faroe Islands, 21
feud and feuding, 2, 21, 25, 41–43, 76
fish and fishing, 20, 25–26, 26, 73, 75, 82, 85, 94
France and the French, 24, 61, 68

game (wild), 25, 26, 30, 31, 85
Gardar (settlement), 37, 40, 41, 79
Germany and the Germans, 10, 24, 45, 48, 65, 74, 76
Gizurarsáttmáli, 53, 92
glacier, 19, 27, 79
goat, 26, 31, 62, 75, 78, 83
Godfred, king of Denmark, 1
goði (goðar, pl.), 38–41, 42–43, 43, 49, 50–52, 54, 91–92
Gorm the Old, 1, 20, 45
Grágás, 3, 4

Hakon Hákonarson, king of Norway, 24–25, 38, 52–54
Hanseatic League, 53, 74–75
Harald "Bluetooth" Gormsson, king of Denmark and Norway, 1, 45–46
Harald Fairhair, king of Norway, 1, 2, 22–23, 25, 32, 37
Haukdælir family, 50–52
Hedeby, 59, 63
Heimskringla, 5
Hekla (volcano), 53, 74
Helluland. *See* North America
Herjolfsnes, 11, 29, 41, 61, 80–81
horse, 26, 30–31, 40, 42, 45, 46, 75, 78, 83

immigrant, 2, 21, 28, 37

immigration, 13
Ingolf, 20–21, 27, 32
Ingstad, Helge and Anne Steine, 3, 5, 78
Inuit, 11–12, 76, 78–79, 80, 81, 84, 85, 93
invasion, 2, 52, 76
Ireland and the Irish, 4, 20, 49
Isleif, 48, 50
Íslendingabók, 3, 20, 27, 48

jarl, 52–53
Jerusalem, 63, 64
John VIII, pope, 20

Kaupang, 59
Ketil Flatnose, 21, 23
knorr, 21, 63, 80

landnám, 20, 21–22, 23, 24, 27, 28, 30, 31–32, 40, 91
Landnámabók, 3, 4, 20, 21, 22, 26, 48, 91
L'Anse aux Meadows, 3, 5, 78
lawspeaker, 39, 40, 41, 46
Leif Erikson, 29, 47–48, 64–65
Lindisfarne, 1
livestock, 19, 20, 25–26, 37, 75, 77, 82, 83
Louis the German, king of East Francia, 20
Louis XI, king of France, 61

Magnus, king of Norway, 53
Markland. *See* North America
medieval, 3, 7, 8, 9, 10, 11, 13, 14, 22, 42, 43, 69, 73, 93
Mediterranean, 59, 64, 92
Middle Ages, 2, 3, 7, 12, 14, 62, 93
monk, 20
monastery, 1, 49

Naddodd, 20, 28
narwhal, 24, 62, 80
Native American, 7, 67, 68, 76; Algonquian, 65, 68; Mi'kmaq, 68
Norðrsetur, 29, 32
Normandy, 63
North America, 2, 3, 5–8, 25, 29, 59, 63, 64–65, 66–69, 76, 78, 85, 92, 93, 94; Baffin Island, 78; Helluland, 69; Labrador, 67, 78; Maine, 67–68;

Markland, 67, 69–70, 78, 92; Newfoundland, 26, 67; Vinland, 3, 7, 8, 27, 29, 60, 64–66, 69, 78–79

North Atlantic: archaeology of, 6, 11, 84–85; geography of, 1, 20, 24–26, 32, 69, 79, 92; history, 8–9, 12, 20, 22, 69; religion, 9–10, 50; sailing and trade, 2, 8, 19, 29, 59, 59–60, 61, 69–70, 73, 75, 91, 94

Norway, 27, 28, 32, 53; geography, 25, 29, 69; kings, 1, 2, 5, 22, 23, 24–25, 32, 37–38, 44, 45–46, 46, 49, 52–53, 62, 68; religion, 5, 9, 45–46, 46–47, 48, 51–52, 92, 93; submission to, 10, 13, 14, 23–24, 24, 41, 54, 59, 73, 79, 91–92; trade and travel, 21, 22, 23, 47, 53, 60, 62, 62–63, 64, 67, 68, 70, 80, 85

Olaf Haraldsson, king of Norway, 1, 9
Olaf Tryggvason, king of Norway, 38, 44–47, 48, 60
Oræfajokul (volcano), 74
Orkney, 21

pagan, 9, 20, 22, 44–45, 46–47, 48, 49
papar, 20, 32
pig, 26
polar bear, 24, 31, 62–63, 82

Reykjavik, 20, 26
Roman Catholic, 9, 31, 45, 48–49, 84
Rome, 49, 63–64
runestones, 45, 50

saga, 3–6, 7, 11, 12, 13, 14, 21, 23–24, 25, 27–28, 38, 38–48, 39, 41, 43, 49, 60–61, 63, 63–64, 66, 68, 76, 91; *Egil's Saga*, 4, 22–23, 26; *Erik the Red's Saga*, 27, 28–29, 47–48, 64–65, 67; *Gisli Sursson's Saga*, 63; *Harald Sigurdarson's Saga*, 64; *Ljósvetninga Saga*, 4; *Njal's Saga*, 4, 43–44, 63; *Saga of Hrafnkel Frey's Godi*, 40–41, 41, 64; *Saga of Olav Tryggvason*, 5; *Saga of Gunnlaug Serpent-Tongue*, 61; *Saga of the Greenlanders*, 29, 48, 64–67; *Saga of the People of Laxardal*, 21, 23, 37–38, 60–61; *Tale of Audun from the West Fjords*, 62–63; *Tale of Halldor Snorrason II*, 64; *Tale of Thorstein Staff-Struck*, 42–43

Scandinavia and the Scandinavians, 1, 3, 6, 8, 9, 13, 19, 20, 22, 25, 26, 28, 38, 44, 48, 50, 53, 59, 61, 67, 69, 74, 77, 91
Scotland, 21
seal, 26, 30, 31, 85
settler, 1–2, 11–12, 19–22, 24–26, 26, 27, 29–31, 32, 41, 46, 47, 49–50, 59, 75, 76, 85, 91, 92, 93, 94. *See also* landnám
sheep, 26, 30–31, 62, 75, 78, 80
Skallagrim, 26
skraelings, 27, 64
Snorri Sturluson, 4, 5, 52, 64
spirit, 47, 66
spiritual, 10, 44
stórgoðar, 52–54
Svein, king of Denmark, 62–63
Sweden, 22, 74

tax, 24, 53
Thing, 39, 40, 41, 43, 91–92; Althing. *See* Althing
Thule: culture, 7, 27, 82; island of, 20

unification, 2

Viking, 1, 9, 11, 13, 19, 20–21, 22, 25, 44, 48, 49, 59, 63, 69
Viking Age, 1, 6, 9, 11, 12, 13, 14, 19, 22, 44, 50, 59, 69, 91, 92
Vinland. *See* North America

walrus, 24, 26, 30–31, 62, 74, 80, 82
war, 2–3, 81, 92, 94
Western Settlement, 5, 29, 49, 67, 74, 75–76, 78, 80, 82, 83
whale, 26, 30, 31

About the Author

Ryan Sines earned bachelor's degrees in history and education from Concordia University Wisconsin in 2007, and a master's in history from the University of Nebraska at Kearney in 2015. He currently teaches middle school at Bethlehem Lutheran School in Sheboygan, Wisconsin. He lives in Sheboygan, Wisconsin, with his wife and two children. Visit his website at www.RyanSines.com.

www.ingramcontent.com/pod-product-compliance
Lightning Source LLC
Chambersburg PA
CBHW031554300426
44111CB00006BA/309